Ripe for Change

HARVARD EDUCATION LETTER
IMPACT SERIES

The *Harvard Education Letter* Impact Series offers an in-depth look at timely topics in education. Individual volumes explore current trends in research, practice, and policy. The series brings many voices into the conversation about issues in contemporary education and considers reforms from the perspective of— and on behalf of—educators in the field.

OTHER BOOKS IN THIS SERIES

Ripe for Change

GARDEN-BASED LEARNING IN SCHOOLS

JANE S. HIRSCHI

HARVARD EDUCATION PRESS

Cambridge, Massachusetts

HARVARD EDUCATION LETTER
IMPACT SERIES

Library of Congress Control Number 2014953101

Paperback ISBN 978-1-61250-771-2
Library Edition 978-1-61250-772-9

Published by Harvard Education Press,
an imprint of the Harvard Education Publishing Group

Harvard Education Press
8 Story Street
Cambridge, MA 02138

Cover Design: Wilcox Design
Cover Photo: Courtesy of Teresa C. Walker
The typefaces used in this book are Chaparral Pro for text and Colaborate for display.

Contents

Foreword

Gardens in schools. Children in gardens. Doesn't this make sense to almost everyone, urban dweller or country cousin, red state conservative or blue state liberal, African American or Latino or Caucasian parents? And yet, if you drive by most schools, what do you see? Expanses of lawn or asphalt, faceless buildings with little hint of students out in the landscape. Once in a while there might be some ornamental shrubs, a bed of daffodils, perhaps a bean teepee. Thankfully, mercifully for students and teachers, this is changing. From Boston to Washington, DC, to Fort Worth to San Francisco, and in lots of city and rural schools in between, school gardening is making a comeback, reclaiming some of that asphalt, helping to build strong bodies (and minds). It's great to have Jane Hirschi's book articulate the ways garden-based learning makes sense. To paraphrase Herbert Hoover (and France's Henry IV before him), Jane makes it clear why we need a garden in every school, and students in each of those gardens.

Ironically, where there seems to be the greatest need, garden-based learning has the fewest institutional footholds to help it survive. *Ripe for Change* shows how change is starting to happen. Jane looks at what it takes for schools, districts, and cities around the country to build real bridges between the garden in the schoolyard and what children experience inside the school.

I've always found inspiration from this statement by American philosopher and psychologist William James: "I am done with great things and big things, great institutions and big success, and I am for those tiny, invisible, molecular moral forces that work from individual to individual, creeping through the crannies of the world like so many rootlets, or like the capillary oozing of water, yet which, if you give them time, will rend the hardest monuments of man's pride."

Let's imagine, all across the country, a legion of tiny, invisible, molecular moral forces creeping through the crannies of the school world. I see teachers, parents, and community members removing chunks of asphalt and then enriching the soil with humus from the school compost pile. I see principals and superintendents pitching in on the weekend to build raised-bed flower gardens for each side of the walkway leading up to the front door. I see sixth graders teaching first graders how to poke a hole in the soil with their pointer finger, plunk a pea into the hole, then cover it with moist soil and wish it well: "I hope you grow, little seed, and feed me peas by the end of the school year." I see school cafeteria cooks running taste tests at lunchtime to introduce third graders to three varieties of beets. I see fourth graders running experiments in their science class to see what proportion of humus and sand makes the best growing matrix for carrots. All this capillary oozing of moral forces can rend the current monument of pride—our unhealthy focus on schools as test score factories.

For too long now, the paradigm has been school as factory, or more recently, school as office. Instead, in the spirit of John Dewey we need to imagine schools as laboratories for democracy, as experimental greenhouses where we figure out the best ways to grow both children and vegetables. Mind you, it's important to grasp that school gardens lead the way to higher test scores and greater student achievement. Jane makes this eminently clear through a survey of all the recent research on garden-based learning. But she also makes it clear that we need to aspire to a "broader definition of success than simply academic outcomes." Time spent in gardens increases students' sense of well-being, improves their attitudes toward the environment, increases their interpersonal skills, expands what they're willing to eat, and provides improved learning for English Language Learners. Gardens can raise test scores *and* make children more active and productive citizens. Now that's a goal worth aspiring to.

It's instructive to realize that garden-based learning is not a new thing; it once flourished in American schools. So what we're actually seeing now is a return to the garden, not some new-fangled educational whimsy. As part of the Nature Study movement at the end of the nineteenth and beginning of the twentieth century, school gardens were heralded as a progressive education innovation that helped "grow a better crop of boys and girls." Innovative schools in Boston, New York, and Philadelphia planted gardens and the idea spread across the country to Cleveland, Dayton, St. Louis, Minneapolis, and throughout California.[1] By 1910 the USDA estimated there were seventy-five thousand school gardens in the country, and two organizations—the School Garden Association of America and the International Children's School Farm League—focused expressly on spreading the school garden movement. Listen to H. D. Hemenway, director of the Hartford School of Horticulture and author of *How to Make School Gardens*, expound the virtues of garden learning: "The school garden creates a love of industry, a love for the country, for nature and things beautiful, and makes boys and girls stronger, more intelligent, truer men and women."[2] Jane's articulation of the benefits of school gardens today is remarkably resonant with the claims being made a century ago! (Though I think she should add "truer men and women" to her list of benefits.)

And so, one wonders, what happened? *Where have all the flowers gone, long time passing?* Where have all those school gardens gone, long time ago? They've gone to the graveyards of mass-market textbooks, No Child Left Behind, standardized testing, mandated time on task, an impoverished view of the big purposes that schools can serve. Even before the educational malaise of the last three decades, schools had become walled off from the nearby natural world. In his provocatively titled article "How My Schooling Taught Me Contempt for the Earth," Bill Bigelow describes his elementary schooling in the 1950s in northern California. "Whether it was in the study of history, writing, science, arithmetic, reading or art, the school erected a Berlin Wall between academics and the rest of our lives . . . The hills above the school were a virtual wilderness of grasslands and trees, but in six years, I can't recall a single 'field trip' to the wide-open spaces right on our doorstep."[3] And I suspect this means that they didn't venture outside into the nonexistent school garden either.

Education, in the last half of the twentieth century, went through a substantial indoor-ification process. The school was Berlin Walled off from the school grounds, gardens, and the nearby community. And the curriculum became less tangible, less hands-on, more abstract. The healthy rebirth of progressivism, of integrated and child-centered curriculum in the 1960s and 1970s, was bulldozed under, starting with the false claims of the *A Nation at Risk* report in 1983. Since then, it's been a downhill trudge into the mire of NCLB and punitive, test-score-driven education policy. *When will we ever learn, when will we ever learn?*

Garden-based education is part of the relearning process and part of the larger movement toward place-based education. Place-based education is about reconnecting schools and communities, classrooms and schoolyards, children and the nearby woods, meadows, and gardens. Reconnecting students with their nearby real worlds makes education more tangible and graspable, which leads to more motivated students. More motivated students are more academically successful. It's a simple formula. Furthermore, in our article "Bring It on Home" in *Educational Leadership*, Greg Smith and I explained that "an education that consists only of the abstract and faraway won't sustain the interest of the young. All young people need to feel that what they are doing makes a difference and contributes to the welfare of others. And all of them need to believe that they can make change. Place- and community-based education provides the perfect context for this work."[4]

The school garden, a nearby "safe but wild place," is one of the best contexts for this work. No field trip permission slips required, no expensive bus rentals, fewer concerns about bathroom facilities. Just down the hall, to the right, and out the door into the schoolyard gardens, where there are weeding and mulching tasks to accomplish, math problems to solve, bugs to identify, a raft of writing prompts, and a vivid experience of making a difference. As Jane clearly articulates, the greater emphasis on contextualized and problem-based learning in the Common Core State Standards aligns beautifully with the garden-based learning opportunities. Higher test scores and truer men and women—what's not to like?

Or, if you have simpler aspirations, the school garden can help here as well. For a number of years, the East Wing at the Westminster Center School in Westminster, Vermont, had a well-entrenched organic-snacks-from-the-garden program. Over the years of growing and putting by dill pickles, dilly beans, grape jelly, tomatoes, carrots, and potatoes, the children honed their math skills, developed critical thinking, deepened their reading and writing abilities, and became more deeply connected with community members.[5] One unanticipated result was that children's tastes changed. A friend of mine, whose daughter was a student there, reported that after a garden-based meal, his daughter came home raving about the delicious vegetables. "Hey, can't we have more Brussels sprouts in our garden? They're so delicious!" Just think: kids who like Brussels sprouts. Garden-based education can make a difference!

—*David Sobel*
Antioch University New England

Garden-Based Learning for a Changing World

At a public school in Cambridge, Massachusetts, preschool teacher Janet Forté has been using her school garden for more than a dozen years. The courtyard garden in the center of this urban school has become an important part of her teaching practice. The growing season in New England may be on the short side, but that hasn't affected the school garden's impact on her students. Nor has it slowed down Janet's garden use as a teacher. Two of her favorite lessons happen after the fall harvest is over and frost has marked the beginning of winter.

Like many teachers in classrooms for young learners, Janet brings a pumpkin into her classroom in October as a tangible emblem of the season and a springboard for fall activities. The class carves the pumpkin into a jack-o'-lantern, counting and saving the seeds—some to toast and taste, and a handful to dry and replant in the spring. But the lesson doesn't end there: in Janet's class the pumpkin stays in the classroom long after other teachers have thrown theirs away. It takes up residence on a tray set on the wide windowsill, and Janet's young students watch as the pumpkin decomposes into a very different form of the jack-o'-lantern they made together a few weeks before.

"It's so interesting and the kids are fascinated by it," Janet notes. "People love to talk about watching things grow, but we don't talk a lot about what happens after things die. And even while this pumpkin is decomposing, there is new life happening. We talk about how there's mold growing on it. We watch it grow and change."[1] After the pumpkin has gotten just about as "saggy and leaky as we can bear," the class brings it to the school's garden coordinator for help burying it in the school gar-

den. Along with the rotting pumpkin on a tray, Janet's class has collected a number of other things they've selected to put in the ground.

> We like to bury [the pumpkin] along with organic and nonorganic things,
> some things that probably will decompose and some things that won't
> and maybe some things in between that we're not sure about. We often
> just pick up things from our snack that day, like apple cores or peel. If we
> had yogurt, we throw in the plastic container, and maybe a spoon and
> some tin foil we find in the classroom. Alison [the assistant teacher] al-
> ways likes to throw in her tea bag. If we've just been talking about leaves
> falling down, we'll grab some leaves, too.
>
> We ask the kids to make predictions: "What do you think is going to
> happen to the pumpkin when we bury it? And each of these things we're
> burying with the pumpkin?" We jot their predictions down, and then we
> put everything all on a tray and go out to the garden to bury it. Very
> methodically, everyone comes and chooses something from the tray and
> drops it in the hole on top of the rotten, liquidy pumpkin.

The pumpkin stays buried until late in the spring when school is almost over for the year. Then Janet and her assistant teachers remind the
children of the pumpkin they buried "so long ago" in the fall. They go out
to the garden and dig it up. The pumpkin and many other things they
buried are gone, but some things are still there—the yogurt container,
the tin foil, the plastic spoon. "It comes full circle and it ties so many
different parts of our academic curriculum together—language, science,
math, how the environment affects us and how we affect the environment, what we eat. Then in the spring, we plant the pumpkin seeds we
saved, and we start all over again!"

The lesson is about much more than nature, Janet points out. It helps
the children think about change in the world and in themselves. It's an
experience that encourages children to talk, to ask questions, to make
predictions, and to learn new vocabulary. "Language is by far the most
important thing we're doing in a preschool classroom. Oral language is
a real indicator for later academic success. So what we're doing is nurturing and helping to facilitate the development of academic language
through real-life experiences. Everyone learns so much better through
having real-life experiences. That will be the bridge to learning from

books and other materials. But in this classroom, the kids need to *live* it," Janet explains.

A GROWING NEED . . .

Janet's preschool class is part of the Cambridge Public Schools district. Over half of the sixteen elementary and middle schools in Cambridge are high needs: they serve a majority of students who are either low income, English language learners, recipients of special education services, or a combination of these. In fact, Janet's class and her school district are not unlike many urban communities with a growing high-need student population, all of whom would benefit from the kinds of lessons Janet draws for her students from her school garden. Hands-on, garden-based learning is also a powerful experience for third graders applying prealgebraic concepts as they track the changes in pea plants growing from March to May; for fifth graders peering into a pollinator garden gone to seed to learn more about plant diversity and ecosystems; or for seventh graders constructing persuasive arguments based on their own experiences in real ecology that feel vitally important to them. In short, the garden is a natural platform for engaging young people in the things we think they should learn.

A garden in the schoolyard presents a visible, welcoming "face" to families and the neighborhood community. It's a place that invites parents to mingle and children to play as they transition between school and home. School gardens soften the contours of schools both physically and psychologically by bringing the institution into harmony with the seasons and the rhythms of the neighborhood.

The garden is also a starting place for children to understand their lifelong dependence on the natural world. A school garden helps children connect to this world through their senses—smells, sights, sounds, and textures—which are so acutely experienced in this outdoor environment. "What might be the most powerful part of the garden for my child and other children is introducing nature without anxiety," a parent of a first grader notes. "In so many ways our children hear about the environment in the context of fear—climate change, animal extinction, air or water or soil pollution. In the school garden, my daughter is introduced to earth science by digging in the soil. She and her classmates develop a personal connection to nature built on their own senses."[2]

When the school garden is also an edible learning garden, as it is in Janet's school, children experience firsthand where food comes from. In the company of their peers, children are more willing to try new and interesting flavors—chives, lettuce leaves, and sungold cherry tomatoes, for instance. Children are naturally cautious eaters, but growing food themselves turns out to be a strong incentive to expand their diet.[3] A child's willingness to eat more broadly because of the school garden is often met with gratitude and surprise by a family concerned about their child's limited vegetable consumption. Sometimes a child's experience in the school garden introduces the whole family to fresh, local produce that had seemed strange and perplexing before.

School gardening efforts vary in size and scope from a single teacher's cluster of butterfly plants to multidistrict, regional programs around the country. "School garden" can mean food production to supplement school meals, food education to promote healthier food choices for children and families, an experiential learning or project-based learning tool for teachers, an ecosystem for observation and exploration, an ambient gathering place for the school community, or a service-learning resource. In practice, school gardens are often a combination of all of these, and they all have the potential for aiding children's learning.

The world has changed in a way that makes the need for school gardens more urgent than ever. The "global village" we now live in gives us access to information and the ability to communicate easily in real time with people on the other side of the earth. Children are growing up with a sophistication about technology that most of us would have found unimaginable even ten years ago. At the same time, important things are lost as our world transforms. Children have less access to nature than they did twenty years ago. Less "free time" and more restrictions on going outside mean that children today have fewer opportunities to explore their neighborhoods even as experts extol the importance of unstructured time for children to play and explore on their own.[4] With shortened recess time in school and fewer opportunities to play outside after school, many urban children's outdoor experience is limited to field trips outside the city, a world away from where they live, learn, and play. Fewer children today are familiar with looking up into the sky, with the subtle signs of weather shifting, with having places to dig and simply noticing things grow and change. The food they eat comes from the store, and a bouquet of flowers is delivered virtually on a computer screen; both are disassociated with a sense of place or season. Children today are facing a different world than what their parents knew, and our communities are being challenged to respond.

Children's experience in the classroom has changed, too. No Child Left Behind legislation, intended to increase student achievement across the board and reduce achievement gaps among student populations, has transformed school culture. Mandatory testing in math and English language arts has reduced the frequency of hands-on, project-based learning in favor of more rote learning that some argue has a closer correlation with higher test results. The intense focus on math and English language arts has decreased the amount of time teachers spend on science instruction, especially in elementary grades.[5] Given the intention of the standards reform to invigorate academic achievement, prepare students for twenty-first-century skills, and erase the achievement gap between well-resourced and less-resourced students, it is ironic that science instruction has shrunk even more for students in schools in low-income communities.[6]

Finally, food systems have changed—often dramatically—affecting everything from the farms and oceans where our food is grown and harvested to the locations where we typically eat. These changes are strongly correlated with a decline in children's health.[7] This has spawned concern not only over children's access to healthy food but also over the fact that they no longer have a base of food knowledge to make good choices about what to eat. Like gaps in academic achievement, the rise of diet-related disease and the decline in access to outdoor play and exploration are particularly acute for children in low-income neighborhoods.

... AND A GROWING SOLUTION

To all of these challenges, garden-based learning is an antidote. Creating gardens in the schoolyard, designed for children to learn from and integrated with teachers' practice, is arguably the most fundamental example of an environment that simultaneously supports children's academic education and their healthy development. Learning gardens and the garden-based learning that happens in them are a natural complement to what current trends in education are calling for. The standards movement that spawned the No Child Left Behind Act in 2001 has evolved again with the widespread adoption of the Common Core State Standards, and while the emphasis on assessment remains unchanged, these newest standards for math and English language arts call for an integration of practice and knowledge with an emphasis on real-world application. The new Next Generation Science Standards emphasize the importance of science in elementary education. They also point to the value of nature experiences as a foundation for students' subsequent science knowledge throughout their elementary and secondary school years. The new standards will change how teachers in many parts of the country are expected to teach. School learning gardens invite a hands-on approach to learning; they are an adaptable medium for a wide range of ages and learning styles. The school garden can be a practical and accessible resource to teachers as they make these shifts.

THE INSPIRATION FOR THIS BOOK

The explosion of garden-based education over the last twenty years has been largely fueled by the efforts of those outside the formal education system. I am among them. In 2000, I was part of a small group of parents, teachers, and a school principal who started a school garden program in Cambridge, Massachusetts. My eldest daughter had just started public school and, like many parents, I was inspired by the example of the burgeoning school garden practice happening around the country. I wanted to help bring edible learning gardens to my city. Our program, CitySprouts, started in two public K–8 schools where a cohort of teachers and the principals were receptive to our grassroots effort. Once we actually began working with teachers and their students, community response to the school gardens was tremendous. Children were enthusiastic. Families were drawn to it. Teachers wanted more. Other school principals asked how and when they could get CitySprouts, too. In short, we experienced what other people around the country were discovering:

from child to adult, people were really hungry for what school gardens promised.

Over the next decade, my role at CitySprouts evolved from volunteer garden coordinator to paid director as the program expanded to all twelve K–8 public schools in the district and then to a handful of public schools across the river in Boston. During that time, I had the good fortune to witness a renaissance of garden-based learning around the country as school garden programs developed to meet the growing need of garden and teacher alike. We witnessed similar outcomes: young people engaged in science; teachers who saw their students learning more deeply, especially noting the impact on English language learners; parents who were convinced their children were eating more vegetables because of what they'd grown and harvested in their garden at school; children, teachers, and parents alike expressing deep affinity for their school garden. As these findings were repeated around the country in diverse school cultures and a variety of schoolyard programs, my colleagues and I considered how garden-based learning could become more accessible to teachers and thus reach more students. If these outcomes were accurate, we agreed, then all children should have access to them, even—especially—in schools that didn't have a parent, teacher, or nonprofit partner to initiate and manage the program.

Schools should be part of how we address the rapid changes in our environment. Within the past fifty years, public schools have undergone a major shift to integrate technology in the classroom. It is equally important today to engage children in the ecology of our natural world. Just as schools are expected to empower children to be active and discerning users of technology, they should also empower children to be actively and discerningly engaged in their natural environment. Opportunities to make healthy food choices, a climate of healthy eating, and a relationship with good food starting from an early age are all correlated with lifelong healthy habits, making edible learning gardens an obvious resource for health education, too.[8]

Across the country, thousands of schools are building and using school gardens.[9] In the absence of comprehensive data about how these school gardens integrate with their school communities and in light of what we know about the demands on classroom teachers' time, we can assume that most of these schools follow the common model where the school garden is the project of inspired parents and motivated classroom teachers who get the garden built and planted, and then make sure that students get to spend time in it. We know as much as we do about the impact of garden-based learning because of the work of these teachers who have spearheaded contemporary garden-based learning efforts in the past twenty years—formal educators like classroom teachers and science specialists but also informal educators like parents and garden coordinators. Often on their own time, these pioneering garden educators have nurtured garden-based learning in our schools.

These pioneers face significant challenges to sustaining garden-based learning in this manner, however. In a culture of standards-based learning, teachers and increasingly other garden educators must identify connections between garden activities and academic learning goals if the school garden is to be part of children's lesson time (as teachers are reminded, "time on task"). In response to the pressure to show how students' time in the garden is relevant to the school's curriculum and learning goals, a handful of garden curriculums have emerged and are used widely, among them Junior Master Gardener, 4H, and Life Lab's *The Growing Classroom*. These curricula have been developed in response to teachers' needs and are often organized by subject area and grade level and aligned with state learning standards. Some offer further resources as well. Life Lab, for instance, provides training for teachers in using their school garden for instruction. Still, most teachers who want to incorporate garden-based learning in school are expected to gather these tools and training on their own time and initiative.

Another hurdle for today's teachers is maintaining the learning garden. All educational resources take time to maintain, of course, whether it's a school library, a robotics lab, or a school garden. In a garden, that includes tasks like watering vegetable and flower beds, repairing irrigation, purchasing tools and supplies, and weeding and harvesting when school isn't in session. Whitney Cohen, Education Director of Life Lab, remembers the experience herself when she was a middle school classroom teacher. "Even if you're weaving it really well into your classroom curriculum . . . even if you're coming out there regularly with your kids to involve them in the garden maintenance and get them into all the learning activities, there will be a lot to do beyond those hours."[10] When the school garden is considered a "special project" rather than a core educational resource in the schools, it depends on volunteer time and skill from teachers, parents, or others in the community to keep garden use alive.

There is a further challenge for teachers in urban, low-resourced schools who are charged with raising struggling students to basic mastery. In high-need schools, there is less time for students and their teachers to spend outside the classroom and away from prescribed math and English language arts curricula. With neither the resources to build a learning garden nor time in the day for children to spend there, these schools and their students are unable to access the benefits of garden-based learning. The "inspired teacher or parent" model that most schools rely on increases the divide between schools that have parents and teachers with the time and means to create and sustain school gardens, and those that don't. Children with the least access to nature, learners most in need of experiential learning opportunities, and those at highest risk for diet-related illness are the least likely to spend time in school gardens. This raises the question of whether school gardens are only for students who have already mastered basic skills or are, in fact, a means to master basic skills.

A CALL FOR CHANGE

There is new, national interest in making garden-based learning more accessible to schools than ever before. The Let's Move campaign, First Lady Michelle Obama's health initiative, includes school gardening as an example of how to "raise a healthier generation of kids." Obama's ongoing partnership with a nearby fifth-grade class to plant and harvest a vegetable garden on the White House lawn is a highly visible symbol for engaging children in growing food and making healthier diet choices. The Farm-to-School initiative in the U.S. Department of Agriculture, funded since 2012, was established to improve both local food procurement in schools as well as food education often associated with school gardens. While these two examples illustrate the school garden's potential for improving health, there are increasing efforts to show its potential for improving academic outcomes, too. Outdoor learning components are being added to nationally used science curricula, for instance, and school gardens are highlighted as a source for potential projects that link ecology and engineering.[11] There are new private/public partnerships supporting garden-based learning in elementary schools around the country, and the body of research on garden-based learning outcomes is accumulating. There is a growing effort to extend the scope of garden-based learning to schools in all parts of the country.

This book looks at the potential for enlarging the scope of garden-based learning in public schools from prekindergarten through eighth grade. Through the examples of five schoolyard programs in cities around the country, I point to ways that urban public schools are exploring how to embed garden-based learning in their school culture. The five stories I tell in this book are just a slice of the big picture of how schools are successfully connecting their students (and teachers and families) with school gardens. The examples I've chosen focus on the work in high-need urban public schools. They describe programs that serve a significant number of schools in a district, if not the whole district (and in one case, *six* districts). Their programs integrate with standards-based curriculum and receive significant public support from the communities they serve; in other words, their "partner schools" are truly partners in the commitment to garden-based learning.

Even though these five stories illustrate only a fraction of all the students and teachers engaged in school gardens, it is an important fraction. I believe that figuring out how to integrate garden-based learning in these high-need urban schools is critical to the long-term sustainability of all school garden programs and their immense benefits for students, whether the focus is health-related, environmental, or academic. This book is meant to help. In the final chapters, I look at national initiatives and policies that have the potential to shape how garden-based education is integrated in public schools moving forward—and ways that educators can help.

Public education will continue to be driven by the question of how to deliver sound academic learning to all children. But schools will also be shaped by our growing awareness of the connection between good health and access to and education about food. Not least, we are searching for ways to take positive action in the face of a frightening environmental crisis: climate change. As a response to all these challenges, we should consider the learning garden.

This book frames current garden education practice and its potential to fully integrate in our public schools. It is intended for an audience that includes current school garden advocates—teachers, parents, outdoor educators—but also educators who haven't yet considered that garden-based learning has the potential to address identified problems in education and children's health. This book is also for principals, school superintendents, and policy makers curious about how their own school or district practice fits into a larger picture of garden-based learning in public education. It is my hope that this book will reach more who are eager to see school gardens and garden-based learning embedded in public schools across the country until all children, wherever they live and no matter their circumstances, experience learning in the garden.

CHAPTER 1

The Origins and Benefits
of School Gardening

Along with the feelings of excitement and hope that accompany garden-based learning is the question of how to ensure that this valuable experience remains available, and equally importantly, becomes much more widely available to many more children. The first hurdle in this dilemma is creating the learning garden itself and making sure that it is maintained. The second issue, which is the primary focus of this book, is how to ensure that children have ongoing and sustained access to learning gardens as part of their school day. While some schools have built in this integration, far too many schools have not. Given that there are 35 million elementary and middle school students in public schools in 2014, that leaves a lot of children without access to the benefits of garden-based learning.[1]

One major challenge to expanding such access is the fact that, while classroom teachers are by and large the gatekeepers to the school garden experience, their discretion over how and what students learn during school time has steadily shrunk over the past twenty years. Thus, the solution is not as simple as just convincing them to make time in the school day for the garden. The decisions most teachers used to make about the curriculum they use, and how and when their students are assessed, are increasingly made by educators outside the classroom at the school, district, or state level. So teachers utilizing their school garden regularly during the school day must establish a very clear connection between garden time and the specific curricula they are required to implement. Not every learning goal is academic, of course—there are also goals for children's health and well-being, for learning to work collaboratively, and for healthy social and emotional development. But the current underlying all of these goals for students is academic, as is made crystal clear by the mandatory assessment in academic achievement to which all public schools are subject. Quite simply, teachers need evidence that time spent in the learning garden is helping their students meet learning goals.

GARDENING AS AN EDUCATIONAL STRATEGY

Fortunately for teachers trying to tie their school gardens to the mandated curricula, garden-based learning in schools has a long history as an educational practice. Teachers approach their school garden, by and large, as a means to teach their students the concepts they need to know in math and science or as an inspiration for writing practice.[2] An appreciation of the wonder of nature and for how food is grown often arises from the foundation of this academic focus.

The garden offers a wealth of things to learn about—the effect of natural cycles and systems, how food is grown, and the role of pollinators and other insects. But the learning garden is more than an area of study. In their interactions with the elements of the garden, children can learn about many things that are highly valued as academic skills. They learn observation and inquiry skills; writing to communicate ideas, directions, and experiences; and math concepts like algebra and geometry. The learning garden is, in the hands of teachers with clear learning goals for their students, a powerful tool for comprehending many things beyond nature study or food production.

In fact, garden-based learning is not even confined to the garden. While it can look like a class of middle schoolers planting and harvesting in the schoolyard vegetable beds or students perched on tree stumps writing in a habitat garden, garden-based learning can also happen inside—for example, students growing plants on the windowsill or observing a decaying pumpkin on a tray. Garden-based learning is less about where a student happens to be in a given moment than using the elements of gardens and growing as a tool that helps children understand a concept or apply a skill. It's a way of learning through the medium of direct experience and reflection, an educational event that engages the senses as well as the intellect. The benefits are not in one experience but rather in the accumulation of them over time. The results of garden-based learning are real and measurable. The benefits accrue with familiarity and experience.

Long ago, teachers undoubtedly turned to the garden for the same reason that teachers continue to use it today: because they perceived that being in the garden helps children learn. Perhaps they saw tangible results, such as improved test scores. Or those early teachers may have been motivated, just like present-day teachers, by the positive changes they saw in their students' behavior: eating healthier food, working collaboratively on group projects, and learning to listen carefully to others. These are all signs of healthy development that educators and parents continue to value today and that are increasingly accepted as important elements of a successful education. In a school day that is packed with expectations for students' measurable improvement, today's teachers use the garden because it produces tangible results.

EXPERIENTIAL LEARNING AND THE PIONEERS OF GARDEN-BASED LEARNING

The educational tradition that allows for this approach to the learning garden is *experiential learning*. In an experiential model of learning, one learns by doing. The teacher's role is to facilitate that process by guiding or focusing students' activity, and then helping them make meaning from the experience. David Kolb describes the process as a cycle that includes direct experience, reflection on that experience, making connections to abstract concepts, and then incorporating understanding of the concept in future experience.[3]

The experiential learning cycle translated to the garden is grounded in children's direct experience helping things grow. They are actively engaged in gardening, but they are also building a familiarity with the complex natural systems in which they are participating. The role of the teacher in this learning process is key, beginning with planning garden activities that present certain concepts or skills; facilitating a meaningful reflection for students about the experience, whether through written word or persuasive speech, to understand math problems, or to apply science concepts; and making sure they have continued opportunities to explore and practice in the garden. Teachers play a critical role by helping students build a relationship with nature as a place they can learn from for the rest of their lives.

Friedrich Froebel

The tradition of educators incorporating the garden as a key part of instruction, and their corresponding role in guiding children's experiential learning, can be traced back at least two hundred years to Friedrich Froebel and the kindergarten movement. Established in Bavaria in the mid-nineteenth century, Froebel's "children's gardens" were meant to be both a literal garden for young children to explore as well as a metaphor to illustrate that a child's healthy physical growth and development could be nurtured just like plants. Froebel believed that through play and exploration in a social, sensory-rich environment, children build a solid foundation for lifelong learning. Strongly influenced by his own childhood experience roaming the woods and meadows in his native Germany, Froebel's philosophy centers on children's self-activity and the teacher's role in guiding it.[4]

Kindergartens today are perhaps the most popular and widespread early childhood institution of education in the United States, with the majority of states providing publicly funded kindergartens to families.[5] They are bolstered by current research that confirms how critical play is for children's development and how much it helps to build cognitive skills, social skills, and the ability to cope with stress.[6] Even when the rationale for kindergarten shifts to reflect educational views focused more on preparing children for formal schooling, many educators still firmly hold that kindergarten is an important place for children's healthy development through play and exploration. Some of the reasons Froebel's teachers incorporated the garden are still true today—the premise that giving children an opportunity to explore is in itself a valuable teaching strategy, and that nature is a primary source of information.

Maria Montessori

More than one hundred years after Froebel, Dr. Maria Montessori extended the assumption that children learn from exploration of the natural world to bring observation and exploration indoors as well as outdoors. The hallmarks of Montessori's approach to education are peer learning, guided choice in activities, and manipulable learning materials designed by Montessori and based on her observation of how children play and learn. Like Froebel, Montessori perceived the teacher's role as supporting children's learning through facilitated, guided exploration. Also like Froebel, she helped establish that discovery and exploration of the natural world was a valid teaching strategy with measurable outcomes.

The impact of Montessori's method has extended beyond Montessori schools to traditional public schools. It is reflected in the practice of learning "stations" set up in the classroom that allow students time to explore and experiment on their own, and in the inclusion of manipulable learning materials in many districts' math curricula. These illustrate the lasting impact Montessori has had on the general public's understanding of how children learn. Montessori's influence is also evident in today's garden-based learning practice in both the role teachers play in facilitating student's learning experience in the garden, as well as in the value placed on students' self-motivation in learning and engagement.

John Dewey

A contemporary of Montessori, John Dewey was a leader in the Progressive Education Movement, which is grounded in the experiential practice of connecting concepts from the classroom to life skills. Dewey insisted that students need opportunities to apply concepts beyond the classroom and in the bigger world, which provides students with hands-on experiences to make lesson content relevant. For Dewey, students' experience in the school garden provided necessary life skills in agriculture (perhaps a life skill valued more for children in the early twentieth century than today). But Dewey also perceived the school garden as a learning environment to study subjects such as math and life sciences. Dewey's theory of education highlights the importance of connecting school to life beyond the classroom walls, and not just for life after graduation but actually as part of the learning process.

Dewey's work coincided with World War I and a rise in the number of urban schools in the United States. Like Montessori, who developed her first schools for poor children in Rome, Dewey was aware that learning gardens had particular value for children without ready access to exploring nature where they lived. *Place-based curriculum*, an iteration of Progressive Education that emerged in the twentieth century, guides children in a deeper understanding of the systems that underlie both environmental and social phenomenon by exploring the communities where they live and go to school. School gardens, while not a necessary condition for place-based education, create rich opportunities for place-based learning. In urban neighborhoods, especially, learning gardens can be a "safe but wild" place for children to explore the environmental and social context of their neighborhoods. Schoolyard learning gardens are a vivid illustration of the connections between the natural systems in the garden and the social networks in the neighborhood. Even in urban communities, children are introduced to such fundamental phenomena as insect life and the impact of weather. Outside in the schoolyard, they see the life of the neighborhood and, with many garden projects, have reason to reach out to neighbors.

EVIDENCE OF A POSITIVE IMPACT

Not only do school gardens offer the opportunity for students of diverse backgrounds to explore and learn from the world beyond the classroom, evidence confirms that they also positively impact students' academic achievement and behavior. In a 2009 summary of the literature on the impact of garden-based learning, Dorothy Blair discusses seven qualitative studies that consider elementary students' learning outcomes from instruction in the garden.[7] Using a combination of methods (e.g., observations, interviews, surveys, and post hoc analysis), these seven studies reveal a range of academic and nonacademic outcomes including an increase in observation skills, math skills, food literacy, parental involvement, a connection to nature, and the recognition of garden-based learning as an effective augmentation to the existing science curriculum.[8]

A more recent survey of garden-based learning literature was conducted by Dilafruz Williams and P. Scott Dixon in 2013. In this comprehensive synthesis of twenty years of research, Williams and Dixon consider forty-eight studies on the impact of garden-based learning on students' academic outcomes.[9] Half were quantitative studies, a little less than a quarter were qualitative, and slightly more than a quarter were a combination. Twenty-two of these studies measured direct academic outcomes like improved grades, increased knowledge, and positive changes in attitudes and behavior. The other twenty-six considered indirect learning outcomes such as healthy eating and physical activity. Studies focused on preK–12 students, with nearly half of the studies looking at students in grades 3–5. Some programs used commercially available curricula and others implemented curricula designed for a specific school. Notably, 90 percent did not report students' ethnicity, 63 percent did not report students' socioeconomic status, and 25 percent did not report whether the school they were studying was public or private.

Overwhelmingly, the studies in both Blair's and Williams and Dixon's analysis show that garden-based learning has a positive impact on elementary students' academic outcomes. In Williams and Dixon's comprehensive evaluation, 93 percent of the twenty-two studies considered saw improvement in science, 80 percent in math, and 72 percent in language arts.[10] Blair concurs that garden-based learning "can improve students' test scores and school behavior."[11] Both sets of authors note the significance of the number of studies that found direct and indirect learning outcomes, reflecting how comprehensive the learning experience in the garden seems to be. They also stressed the lack of rigorous procedures in the studies overall and emphasized the need for further research. Program evaluations of garden-based learning in Boston Public Schools, Cambridge Public Schools, and public schools in Texas (reported in detail later in this book) also confirm that students who participate in science lessons with their teachers outside in the schoolyard do more active investigating and observing. Over seven hundred elementary students in Boston were found to exhibit more curiosity and use more science vocabulary than do students who study science only inside the classroom; the Boston students also indicated higher interest in and confidence about their science skills and knowledge.[12] In short, there is a wealth of evidence confirming that school gardens do indeed provide an experience that positively impacts the very elements that make students successful.

A Spark That Engages

The school garden has a positive impact on student success in part because there are so many different ways it can pique a child's interest and senses: meeting the world of insects that every garden contains, feeling the excitement of the changing light (and sometimes weather) through the day and seasons, tasting new flavors. The garden offers children lots of entry points. New evidence suggests that even very young children enter school with more knowledge about the natural world than educators had previously thought, implying a ready base of experience—and interest—that garden-based learning helps teachers build on.[13] Further, a child's interest and enthusiasm in the science of the natural world can lead to a deeper participation in learning and positively influence later educational and career choices.[14] A resource such as a learning garden, in other words, is a great boon to teachers tasked with finding environments that will consistently engage most, if not all, of the students in their class. Teachers have noted that garden-based learning is particularly beneficial for students who aren't fluent in English by helping them retain what they learn.[15] For English language learners, hands-on learning lowers the language threshold and allows them to approach a concept or skill on a more equal ground with their peers who are fluent in English. As our public school demographic becomes increasingly diverse, more and more teachers will need to be ready to meet this challenge.

Finally, children's full and healthy development includes academic learning but also much more. Recent studies on garden-based learning indicate that students' time spent in the school garden increases their sense of well-being, improves their attitudes toward the environment, and increases their interpersonal and cooperative skills. Garden-based learning in edible school gardens expands what foods children are willing to try and has even been linked to changes in students' food choices and attitudes toward healthy food.[16] Such nonacademic outcomes shouldn't be separate from the valuable academic achievements we hope all children gain from school. Today's learning gardens, aligned with the philosophy underlying kindergartens, reflect a broader definition of success than simply academic outcomes.

A Resource for Nondominant Learners

It may be clear that all children benefit from garden-based learning, but it is also true that, as noted earlier, for some children the need for such a resource is especially acute. Gaps in achievement among demographic student groups have plagued our public school system for decades. Recent studies on how children learn show that children entering school for the first time bring with them very different sets of experiences that affect their school success right from the beginning. Race and ethnicity, language, culture, gender, and socioeconomic status all impact children's ability to succeed at the tasks schools expect them to do.[17] Further, the "resource gaps" with which children begin school are likely to continue throughout their school years. While children experience some of these resource gaps at home, they also experience them in our school system. In schools that struggle to make adequate yearly progress, the focus on testing can further decrease these students' access to engaging, intellectually challenging instruction. Their schools are less likely to have the resources for informal learning experiences, such as field trips to museums, parks, or farms. They are also less likely to have a learning garden in their schoolyard.

To these students, the learning garden is particularly important. In the garden, they can start to build the inquiry skills they may not have developed prior to school. They accumulate the kinds of nature experiences that research shows is a necessary foundation for science literacy. In short, they get hands-on learning and a whole host of experiential learning practices that are not currently available to underresourced schools and communities. Yet even as school garden programs are increasing around the country, they are not reaching children in these underresourced communities. The limits on teachers' time and schools' focus on children's academic outcomes mean that most school gardens still rely on parents, volunteers, and inspired teachers to keep them going. It's clear that the wealth of outcomes associated with garden-based learning is not yet sustainable for many schools.

THE SCHOOL GARDEN AS A POWERFUL TOOL

The experiential learning tradition is the container for contemporary garden practice. The school garden, in turn, has been a resilient tool for the practices at the heart of experiential learning. It has consistently provided a good environment to nurture and build on a child's natural curiosity, a place for the teacher to guide children's learning experience, and a vivid example that by engaging children we can help them become invested in their own learning. Kindergarten, the Montessori method, and Progressive Education illustrate how the school garden has long been an important resource for teachers in engaging children, teaching them vital knowledge about the world, and introducing necessary life skills as they grow into adulthood. These examples show that an academic approach to garden-based learning can in fact be a catalyst to a wealth of critical nonacademic benefits. Learning about how food grows and academic instruction in the garden are not mutually exclusive by any means.

Dorothy Blair captures the power of the garden for children that shines through the many research studies. "Each year, students could be full participants in designing the garden and the act of regeneration, the regenerative act of embedding tiny seeds in dirt and food-scrap compost, and nurturing those seeds during their transformation into flowers or vegetables," she writes. "Researchers have frequently commented on how excited children were to put their hands in dirt."[18]

Montessori's elucidation of the concept that students learn better when they are *engaged through doing* is acknowledged by contemporary educators as a powerful factor in how children learn. The outcomes Dewey associated with garden-based learning have come back around one hundred years later as twenty-first-century skills: we see renewed interest in fostering children's creativity and innovation, critical thinking and problem solving, communication and collaboration.[19] Using the learning garden for instruction has emerged as an incredibly important tool precisely because it is such an effective way for children to learn. It ties knowledge and application in ways that make inherent sense to children, strengthens teachers' practice, and bolsters the argument for experiential learning. It places garden-based learning on a firm foundation as an educational practice, making it much more possible that all children will begin to get access to learning gardens through their classroom teachers because it creates a place in the school day—and in teachers' practice—for children to explore the wonders of nature. And from that experience, many wonderful things can begin to grow.

CHAPTER 2

What Learning Looks Like in the Garden

MAKING CONNECTIONS
ACROSS SUBJECTS AND GRADE LEVELS

Without an explicit requirement to incorporate the school garden into academic lessons and often without much support in terms of preparation or supplies, teachers are still making the garden part of where and how they teach. They are integrating garden-based learning into lesson plans, organizing the class for lessons outside, and finding ways to connect their students' outdoor learning experience to the curriculum back in the classroom. Teachers in all schools, but especially in high-need schools, must plan these lessons within the scope and sequence of their core academic subjects. Teachers are mindful of how critical their choice of class activities and projects can be for students struggling to master reading, writing, math, and science concepts. They perceive the school garden as a key tool in teaching the academic skills and content they're responsible for imparting. For them, the classroom extends beyond the walls of the building to include the garden in the schoolyard.

These teachers have discovered that the school garden is uniquely suited to help children learn. It provides a context for understanding both simple and complex concepts (volume and area, for instance), tracking changes over time, and distinguishing between biotic and abiotic. It is a place where students practice skills like measurement, scientific observation, informative writing, and poetry. Of course, these are skills that can be taught in many ways, but teachers find that the school garden is a particularly engaging environment for their students. Garden-based learning can bridge academic subjects in a way that not only imparts skills and content but also helps students understand why these skills are important and how they can be useful. Further, the edible learning garden allows teachers to "fold in" health and food education without competing with core academic time. The schoolyard garden is a sensory-rich change in environment from the classroom, and it is just outside the door.

Teachers point out that the value of the garden experience increases as students spend more time in it. So a challenge for teachers is to plan garden lessons that don't stand alone but rather are part of a series of visits that allow students' garden experience to accumulate. For a child's learning to flow seamlessly from classroom to garden, a teacher must identify multiple points where the curriculum connects to the garden. These multiple opportunities to take lessons outside offer teachers a way to both help their students understand a concept or practice a skill and to still be sure they've covered "what's on the test." Even a modest garden comprising a few raised beds and a compost bin in an urban schoolyard provides ample opportunity for children to see things happening, to get excited about writing, and to practice observing or using their reasoning and creativity to make sense of the complex systems in nature. A teacher may begin using the garden based on an intuition that this is a valuable experience for students, and then discover multiple curriculum connections to not only justify, but *demand*, a deeper commitment to garden-based learning.

TEACHING SCIENCE IN THE LEARNING GARDEN

A report from the National Research Council confirms that children learn science by doing it and further, that a range of approaches is necessary for children to understand science.[1] The connections for science knowledge are strongest in the life sciences—plant growth, soil, living and nonliving things, for instance—but science skills such as observation, inquiry, and problem solving are natural and obvious connections to every area of science, and at every grade level.

Susan Agger, a science specialist in Cambridge Public Schools, describes a seventh grader who surprised her with his knowledge of the fauna in his urban environment. He had first learned about the common cabbage white butterfly (*Pieris rapae*) in the school garden four years earlier when he was a third grader. Now, he told Susan, "I see them all the time when I'm on the field at football practice." Since first learning about the butterfly, he had learned the names of all kinds of insects that he noticed as he went about his day. An initial experience, not even a formal part of the lesson, had sparked this boy's curiosity and initiated his personal four-year project to build a body of knowledge about the natural world around him. "Kids do see a lot in the city, and they do make a connection," Susan says. "They're building outdoor experience. That's one of the greatest values of the garden . . . it's often where those initial, personal experiences are going to happen. There's always something that they notice on their own that they're going to be curious about. I think kids' natural curiosity is really valuable. And in the garden, they can't help but be curious! It pulls them along."[2] Not infrequently, spending time in the school garden helps deepen students' observations, as it did for this young man who continued asking questions and looking for answers long after the initial garden experience was over.

Recent research shows that, contrary to previous thought, most children begin school with significant knowledge of the natural world, even if they don't have the language to describe what they know.[3] Kindergarten teacher Neal Klinman notes that for his students the school garden differed from more general outdoor education because they spent enough time in the garden to become really familiar with it, and that in turn helped his students become more adept at observation. "We could just walk around the neighborhood and look at the beautiful colors, but [instead] we keep going back to the garden from the summer to the autumn, and we see the changes. It's inspiring to go out and see the kids *really looking*."[4] The practice of really looking and the opportunity to come back to the same place to notice how it changes over time not only expands students' base of knowledge, it also teaches them skills they will need throughout their education, in English language arts as well as in science.

Deep observation in the garden connects to language, to naming and describing what one sees and experiences. Improving students' literacy, developing their speaking skills, and expanding their scientific vocabulary are all goals that teachers find the school garden helps them meet.

"We very pointedly integrate [garden time] with literacy, introduce math concepts . . . we're trying to weave it together," explains Neal. "It's more than just exploring. To make it more rigorous, we take our science notebooks. We look at the color words and how to spell them, copy some of the text from the signs in the garden, utilize the alphabet garden along the fence, give attention to cooperation as kids work in teams and have a job to do together . . . those are all really important skills to practice." Garden-based learning is an effective means to help children put words to their growing knowledge of nature.

Spotlight on Third Grade

Understanding the role that plants play in ecosystems is a key concept in life sciences and a standard unit in elementary science curricula. Wisconsin Fast Plants (*Brassica rapa*) have been widely used in classrooms since 1987 to show students the full cycle of a plant's development through all its stages.[5] From planting to flower, the Fast Plant matures in only two weeks, giving classroom teachers a nearly foolproof method for demonstrating a plant's life cycle—and one that conveniently fits in a teacher's typical scope and sequence timeline. Traditional *Brassica* varieties, on the other hand—broccoli, collard greens, and kale, for instance—take a full season to mature and are not as well adapted to life on a windowsill.

Third-grade teacher Kelly Petitt teaches Plant Growth and Development every spring. As part of that unit, Kelly's third graders plant Wisconsin Fast Plants in the classroom. Most of Kelly's third graders are unfamiliar with seeing plants grow in gardens; there just aren't that many backyard gardens in the dense, urban neighborhoods where they live. Their school has a learning garden, however, and Kelly has devised a way to incorporate the garden to expand her students' concept of plant life. On the same spring day that her students plant the Fast Plants inside, they also plant kale outside in the school garden. Within a few days, they observe the cotyledon leaves on the Fast Plants, and very soon after that the Fast Plant buds develop. Each day they also take a walk outside to the schoolyard garden to examine the place where they planted their kale seeds. Not until the Fast Plants already have flowers do they start to see the first signs of germinated kale seeds unfolding in the garden soil. "Their minds are blown to have that comparison to an actual plant life cycle!" Kelly says. But what they get from that comparison is more than plant-part knowledge; they experience firsthand the impact of the environment on plants growing under natural conditions. The comparison between slow growth outside and speedy growth inside drives home the fact that plants can be bred for very particular conditions.

Taking a full class of twenty-five to thirty students into the learning garden requires strategies and forethought. "You have to have a really strong sense of what you want to happen when you take kids outside," Kelly explains. "What you want them to be doing, where you want them to be. It's different, and it's really exciting for them. What I often do at the beginning of the year is to go outside just to let the kids explore. So we go out to the garden and we observe it. We sit and listen and smell . . . 'what do we notice in the garden?' I spend a couple of sessions letting them know the expectations, starting when we're inside. Then they can explore and poke around on their own." [6]

Like the seventh grader whose introduction to a common butterfly in the learning garden sparked an interest that was still going strong four years later, or a kindergartener who begins to put words to her experience of the natural world, Kelly's third-grade students are building their capacity as learners through the school garden. "I want my third graders to leave me at the end of year knowing all of the content that I'm responsible for but also what to do if you want to know something," Kelly explains. "If there's something that you want to know, how do you go about finding out the answer . . . how do you test it out for yourself? I let them choose where they're going to look for things growing. And sometimes when they don't find things growing, it's as powerful as when they do find it . . . It's helping kids see that you're learning things that will serve [you] your whole life."

Spotlight on Middle School

The majority of garden-based learning happens in the elementary grades, but that's not to say that the learning garden doesn't have value for older students, too. In fact, the edible learning garden is particularly beneficial in meeting the unique academic and social challenges young people face in these years.[7] The ages between eleven and fourteen are a particularly vulnerable time for young people as they transition from childhood to teenage years, not firmly embodying either. Students' future academic course is often charted in these critical years. In addition, as they gain more autonomy over their food choices, they establish eating habits that often take them into adulthood, if not through their whole lives. Most obviously, they are particularly sensitive, often vulnerable, to peers in both healthy and unhealthy ways.

Donna Peruzzi and Madhvi Patil are two middle school science teachers in Cambridge who have found ways to integrate their school learning garden in their science curriculum. Donna teaches genetics to seventh and eighth graders every fall. She uses the garden to help her students understand plant reproduction by looking for sexual and asexual examples among the plants. The lesson begins in the classroom when Donna gives a short introduction to explain the two different ways that plants reproduce and makes sure her students know what indicators to look for once they're outside. "Then," Donna says, "we go out looking for them. Once kids figure it out—'oh, flowers mean sexual reproduction!'—it gets easier."[8] Strawberry plants are an example of both sexual (via the flowery sexual organs) and asexual (the runners, or stolons). "I loved going to the strawberry patch because that's where we see both. I point out one or two of the runners; then kids would look for others." Until recently, Donna taught this unit in the spring, when students had an opportunity to see the small, still-green strawberry fruit forming in the center of the flower. Yet when her district moved the unit to the fall, she discovered that the fruits and flowers in the fall garden still provided adequate examples for her students to explore the difference between sexual and asexual plant reproduction. Donna notes that visual examples of plant reproduction are increasingly accessible to her as a teacher through technology in her classroom. Yet she feels that physically being in the garden on a "scavenger hunt" for plant reproduction indicators is much more engaging for her students. "It's like a mini–field trip, but no permission forms needed! Being out there just makes it so much more memorable."

Students bring their science journals with them to the garden to draw and describe what they find and to write down any questions they have. Back in the classroom, Donna uses her students' questions as prompts for further discussion. "Kids will see different things. I keep it open where they go, so long as they are on the paths and not stepping on the plants. If they're drawn to different parts of the garden, they're going to see different things. Even though I want it to be flexible, I still want them all to understand we have a purpose for being out there." Taking this lesson to the garden gives Donna's students a vivid example of a basic biological principle. It's also a concept that is likely to be asked on the state science assessment, Donna notes. As her students review material later in the school year, Donna tells them to "remember the strawberry patch." It's an anchor experience that helps them retrieve the material they need to know.

Madhvi is a seventh-grade science teacher at a Cambridge middle school across town. She uses her school learning garden to illustrate the transfer of energy through matter, a theme running through her seventh-grade curriculum. The garden helps her students understand the concept of energy when they see its impact: how the energy from the sun is stored in plants or seeds (matter) throughout the winter and is then released as they resume growing in the spring. "It's all in the roots, actually," Madhvi explains. "That is the most important thing in that short period of time, to grow a root system. Basically what happens is the leaves come out, they make their sugars, and then they are all stored in the root for the next time around. Frost comes and the plant goes into hibernation, but life stays in the root."[9] Because her students grow a variety of grains in their school garden, Madhvi also uses the lesson to reflect on the impact that plant diversity has historically had on food systems.

Garden-based learning, Madhvi finds, helps her seventh graders stay connected to new concepts introduced in middle school by grounding them in a context that they are familiar with and comfortable in: the school garden. It's not uncommon for middle school students to lose interest in science or feel like they can't master it, Madhvi notes. Her students are being introduced to physics, chemistry, and a more sophisticated level of life science than what they were used to as elementary students. Part of Madhvi's job is to keep her students engaged in the face of these challenges, and she uses her school garden to help her do that. The garden, she points out, "is accessible to students of all levels in the classroom. They can understand what's happening, they can do it—and that's confidence!" Her students come from elementary schools with school gardens (CitySprouts is the districtwide school garden program), so Madhvi uses their familiarity with the learning garden to introduce them to the more demanding middle school curriculum. It also helps Madhvi explain the relationship between the three seventh-grade science units she teaches by "keeping energy and matter constant through those units." Madhvi would like to see technology incorporated into her students' garden experience as a means for students in different schools to share information and results about what they're learning in the garden. Technology, in Madhvi's view, is not an alternative to garden-based education but rather a potential enhancement to it.

The learning garden has other benefits for middle school students beyond the academic connection. Donna searches for a word to describe the particular mind-set of this "in-between" age: "*Unpredictable* comes to mind, even in the same child from one day to the next," she finally settles on, laughing. "But still curious. They have this battle of wanting to be responsible for things and be treated like an adult but also not wanting too much responsibility . . . they still want to play! They have some ideas of what they think about things, but they're not too old to change their minds." Learning in the garden is important for her students, she continues, "because they're still in that transition, they still need opportunities for that outdoor . . . almost *play*. They don't get as many times to be outside. If I can build in just five minutes for them to relax at the end of the lesson, I think that's important. For many kids in an urban environment, just being outside under a tree and in the grass is just not often happening for them anymore. Whether they're inside playing video games, or outside on an asphalt court playing basketball, [being in the garden] is just a different experience from their day-to-day lives."

TEACHING WRITING IN THE LEARNING GARDEN

Arguably, nothing is more valued in schools than fluency in reading and writing. Because a significant portion of writing instruction is usually based on material that students generate, and because students who are engaged in their topic often find more to say about it, teachers seek out environments and experiences that inspire students' reflection. Teachers turn to the school garden for all kinds of writing. They use the sensory-rich school garden as a focus for descriptive writing like poetry and narrative. Planting, harvesting, and eating become springboards for explaining sequences clearly (*first, then, last*). Students learn informational writing by recording observations and questions in their science journals. They create math word problems based on practical tasks in the garden, such as how many garlic bulbs can be planted in a given space, or how much soil it will take to fill a new raised garden bed. Writing in the garden helps to connect literacy to subjects that have traditionally been taught separately, such as building scientific vocabulary or making persuasive arguments. The learning garden provides a practical reason for teachers to expand the amount of informational reading students do throughout their elementary and middle school years by making literacy a more explicit expectation in science and social studies. In other words, in the learning garden students not only read to know, they also write to tell.

Spotlight on First Grade

First-grade teacher Caitlin O'Donnell has been using her school garden for several years. At first, the lessons Caitlin taught in the garden were extensions of her science units. Her students made lists of living and nonliving things they found in the garden, for instance, or explored the compost for worms and other decomposers. Over time, however, Caitlin shifted the focus of her students' time in the learning garden to writing instruction. "I started moving toward just letting kids have more experiences in the garden even if it wasn't related to a science standard or a social studies standard. Any of those experiences [in the garden] are rich fodder for writing, and not just science writing. It's a different experience that a lot of kids just don't have in their daily lives. As a teacher, I do Writers Workshop every day," she explains. "You may write in a variety of genres but to all of that, kids need to bring some material—some ideas."[10]

Every week, Caitlin schedules time to take her class out to the garden. With the garden coordinator's assistance, she often divides the class into two smaller groups or "stations." One group might dig in a garden bed looking for worms and other insect life. The other group might plant (garlic in the fall, for instance, or salad greens in the spring), harvest a variety of herbs to taste back in the classroom, or sift compost from the bin and then add it to a garden bed. The activities the first graders do in the garden become topics for morning meeting or writing time, or simply points of reference during science back in the classroom. "It means that every week the kids have stories to tell *and that they could write about*, looking for worms, pulling up the stakes, making apple cider," Caitlin says. "To dig, water, to do the work of a gardener in their own way . . . that's what brings action to their stories. They're urban kids and they might not get to have experiences with plants and dirt and insects at home."

Garden time has increasingly become a source of material for Caitlin's classroom instruction. For some children, the garden experience is a critical point of engagement necessary for a literacy assignment. Caitlin described one such time, when a student's deep interest in the garden helped her find a reason to write a personal narrative in the Writers Workshop curriculum Caitlin uses. "She was a reluctant writer . . . she just wasn't into 'small moments,'" Caitlin remembers. "She was a smart kid and very articulate, and she was totally obsessed with the garden. Every day she'd discover something new. She loved to know the names of the plants. So when it came time to write our nonfiction "All About" books and she realized she could write about the garden, she was really motivated, [was] really productive, and wrote a wonderful book with lots of illustrations. It was a great book and a great experience for her to discover something she was knowledgeable about." For this young girl, the garden gave her a reason to write.

Garden-based learning can also provide valuable opportunities for children to practice speaking skills. Caitlin's students enter her classroom with a broad range of ability levels, including in communication competency. Like many teachers, Caitlin finds that the garden facilitates important communication and interpersonal skills: being able to work in groups, to listen to ideas and then explain them, and to integrate information from a variety of media, such as the complex and engaging medium of natural phenomena.[11] Caitlin has found that working in the garden creates rich opportunities for conversation and for vocabulary development. "It makes a difference to talk while they're working," she says. "'Let's see if we can find some roots,' or 'let's see what we can find that's living and nonliving while we're digging in the soil.' You can have a discussion about it right there."

Garden writing prompts can happen inside the classroom, too. At the beginning of the year, Caitlin's students helped tend the corn growing in a small raised bed next to the playground. Later in the fall, they harvested the popping corn with Greg, the garden coordinator at their school. Then, on a mid-winter afternoon, Greg visited the classroom with the now-dried corn. Greg reminded the students that the corn came from their garden. He explained how there was moisture in the hard kernels, and when they got hot the kernels burst open into popcorn. The students helped Greg get their corn ready for the popper and witnessed the transformation for themselves. "We pulled the kernels off like wiggly teeth—something first graders know really well," Caitlin says. "We put them in the popper—it was super exciting! Then we ate it." Later that week, Caitlin built a writing lesson around the experience.

The popcorn activity tied in a number of key concepts for Caitlin's students. First, the harvested corn reminded students of their time in the garden throughout the fall. They observed how the dried corn changed from a plant in the garden to something they can eat. They learned how corn can transform again from a hard, yellow seed to puffy white popcorn. They celebrated their harvest with popcorn as the special treat. Lastly, Caitlin used it all as a prompt in her writing lesson on explaining events in sequence. "We were doing procedural texts then, and it worked out really well to think about what the steps would be."

MAKING CONNECTIONS TO EDIBLE EDUCATION

Teachers approaching their school gardens for academic instruction also recognize the edible education that happens in the learning garden even when it's not the focus of the lesson. Teachers who have made the school garden integral to their standards-based lessons still find time for tasting and eating and talking about food.

In Kelly Petitt's garden lesson, the focus is on plant science. Kelly directs her students' attention to the content: understanding the stages of plant growth, for instance, and the impact of the environment. But she is well aware that they are also learning about food by planting kale.

Her students will get the opportunity to taste it before school lets out in June, and many of them will harvest the mature crop in the fall. "When we're out in the garden and getting our hands dirty, it really solidifies that connection that plants grow from seeds. To see that and have that ownership is really powerful, and they start to build that connection with where food comes from. Kids are so disconnected about how their food gets to them," she added. "Being able to do this here in our garden and, in a broader sense [learning that] there are people growing food all over the world, makes it real for them. It's about knowing how the world works. Food comes from farms and gardens—that's important for them to know."

In garden-based learning, tasting can become so intertwined with the rest of the garden experience that it almost becomes invisible. But that doesn't make it less powerful. "How many of them would be eating chives if they weren't picking them in the garden?" Caitlin asks about her first graders. "They're obsessed with chives! I think it's because they actually have an interesting flavor and it tastes like something. And," she adds, "they can name it."

In Donna Peruzzi's school, the garden is right outside the cafeteria. Students can see it from their lunch tables. For the past several years, her school has participated in cafeteria composting, where food waste is collected and trucked to a compost processing facility. While students don't see the actual composting of their school food waste, she's sure that they have a better understanding of the process from having composted on a small scale in their school garden.

There is also the benefit of simply giving students more time outside. Neal Klinman is aware of just how important this is for urban children. "Even living in the city you can see the changes in the seasons, looking at the trees . . . but there are some kids who really, literally, never get a chance to run their fingers through the dirt," he says. "And even if they *do* get that opportunity, most kids want more! Somebody who has a garden at home wants to bring their experience, their expertise, to school. And kids who don't have that at all get a chance to get dirty and sift through a worm pile or shuffle through the leaves."

LOWERING THE LEARNING THRESHOLD SO EVERYONE CAN ENTER

The richness and diversity found in the school garden, supported by a well-designed lesson and a skillful teacher, helps students of varying levels of proficiency and interests get engaged in a deep way. For children who start school without the tools to help them succeed—less exposure to reading, science, and numeracy; or lacking a robust "school vocabulary"—garden lessons give them a chance to practice these skills in an environment that builds on their prior knowledge and pulls them right in. For older students transitioning to middle school, it helps them stay engaged as they meet new academic and social challenges.

Increasingly, teachers have to plan lessons for students with a wide range of skill levels and very diverse experience. In Cambridge, Massachusetts, where Neal, Caitlin, Kelly, Donna, and Madhvi teach, the six-plus square miles that make up the city include Harvard University and MIT. While many students in Cambridge Public Schools have access to the resources associated with these institutions, not all of them do. Of the six thousand students in the district, more than 40 percent live below the poverty line, 32 percent speak a language other than English at home, and 20 percent are on special education plan for learning disabilities.[12] As Caitlin says, "I have a very diverse class. The garden gives us a common experience that we can all talk about."

Learning gardens can be an important resource for teachers facing an increasingly diverse student population precisely because they integrate three key elements of health, learning, and environmental literacy. They give students exposure to new foods, an understanding of where food comes from, and an introduction to food systems. Like environmental education, particularly place-based education, school gardens integrate the natural world and local community *and at the same time facilitate meaningful understanding of academic concepts.* Garden-based learning addresses needs particular to students in urban neighborhoods and typical in high-need schools.

More fundamentally, however, teachers are using their school gardens in ways that reflect strategies accepted as best practices for all students: engaging students in their own learning, approaching learning as development, and integrating knowledge with practice. The learning garden offers a valuable opportunity to engage these practices, and an opportunity right outside the classroom door. "Teachers shouldn't say, 'I need to go to the garden,' but rather 'I need to teach this math concept and the garden will give my students a chance to both learn it *and* apply it,'" Dan Monahan, a science educator, explains.[13] In other words, garden-based education might be an opportunity too valuable *not* to have.

CHAPTER 3

Barriers to Integrating Gardens in Schools

The work that garden-using teachers are doing and its impact on students' learning should be an impetus for educational leaders and policy makers to find ways to embed garden-based learning systematically so that it can reach more students, everywhere. Whether teachers "dip" into the school garden to supplement a lesson or plan extended projects, the learning garden is a place students get to know over time, where their knowledge deepens and their curiosity is encouraged. It is a way for students to make sense of what they learn in the classroom, and an opportunity for them to practice skills by applying them to real situations. It is also a way for many more children to experience edible education as part of their school day.

Like the start of many good practices, these teachers' results should be the catalyst for a shift in expectations. Why shouldn't all schools have gardens? Why shouldn't all teachers have the support to utilize garden-based learning? And why don't all children get to experience the powerful impact of learning in their school garden?

Despite the fact that teachers are indeed integrating learning gardens to positive ends, there are nevertheless big challenges that hinder this work and prevent all children from getting the benefit of garden learning. Teachers in Cambridge echo many of the challenges cited by teachers around the country, confirming that there are consistent barriers to connecting our children with garden-based learning in public schools. These obstacles start with a lack of time, both to take students outside for a lesson as well as to prepare for it. Teachers' efforts are further obstructed when their district-mandated curriculum has no obvious connections to the experiential learning the garden offers. Lastly, teachers cite the lack of purposeful garden design, adequate maintenance, and available support staff as challenges to integrating garden-based learning. They know they need a resource that they can count on (and plan for) when they go outside with a class of twenty-five to thirty excited young gardener-students.

This chapter details these challenges that teachers commonly identify as barriers to integrating garden-based learning more fully into their classrooms. In the following chapter, we will see how five different districts have begun to address these issues and how this accumulated knowledge is pointing the way toward best practices.

LACK OF TIME

Teachers consistently say that a lack of time is a challenge to their garden-based learning practice. Data gathered from teachers who use the garden, and also from those reporting why they don't, shows that teachers' limited control over the hours of the school day impedes their deeper, more consistent use of the school garden.[1] In fact, teachers struggle with even fitting district curriculum requirements into the school day, much less garden-based lessons and projects. "If you add up all of the minutes that all of the departments are requiring teachers to put into the school week, it's way more than the school day that we actually have, especially given transitions and other things that matter, like helping kids with their interpersonal problems or their family issues or their trips to the nurse, or the healthy snacks that we're trying to do. It's challenging to fit things into that schedule," one teacher notes.[2]

With the minutes of the school day so tightly scripted, the time it takes teachers to transition their class to the outdoor learning garden, even when it's right outside the classroom, can pose a challenge. Even more basically, it takes time for teachers to develop and integrate garden-based learning into their practice. Teachers need to figure out how to plan a meaningful garden extension to their curricula. Returning to David Kolb's experiential learning cycle (described in chapter 1), the teacher's process often begins with planning an experience in the garden focused on a specific learning goal, which entails either the teacher or a support staff member considering what children will actually find in the learning garden—the variety of living and nonliving things to discover—compared to coverage of the same unit inside the classroom. It means organizing a whole class for a lesson outside and then facilitating the activities that lead children to reflect on the experience back in the classroom. Finally, it involves setting up additional garden visits to give students an opportunity to practice what they've learned, since research shows that meaningful learning needs "sustained opportunities" for deep and long-term comprehension.[3] This assumes that teachers using the garden have a solid familiarity with the lesson content they're teaching as well as the outdoor learning space. If a school or district hasn't secured this time in teachers' scheduled professional development, then the teachers must find this time on their own.

NO BRIDGE TO THE CURRICULUM

The challenge of time can be at least partly ameliorated when curriculum is designed from the outset for learning experiences like the garden. Teachers' task, then, is to identify where in their given curricula an activity or project in the garden would enhance their students' engagement with or comprehension of a concept or skill. The more clearly these curriculum connections are identified, the more teachers are able to incorporate garden-based learning. Depending on the choices schools and districts make about their curriculum, garden-based education can be easier or more difficult for teachers to actually implement. It's not terribly difficult to find such connections in many states' learning standards, but as more and more school districts determine the curricula teachers must use in the classroom, alignment with standards is less important than alignment with a particular curriculum's scope and sequence. That can present real challenges to teachers trying to integrate the garden. For instance, Kelly Petitt made a meaningful enhancement to the plant growth science lesson her district uses by planting *Brassica* seeds outside in the learning garden as well as inside the classroom. But these enhancements can happen only if her plant growth unit coincides with the planting season, or if Kelly has the leeway to decide when to teach that unit.

The importance of aligning with curriculum continues all the way to the point of assessment and how much state tests measure the outcomes that garden-based learning delivers: experiential learning, integration of subject areas, and hands-on opportunities for students to apply concepts and practice skills. Teachers (and many other educators, too) express concern about how current assessment processes fail to capture the depth and breadth of learning that they know are necessary for children's development. While not a concern limited to the school garden, it encompasses all of the informal learning environments educators know children should be exposed to. Unfortunately, current assessment of students' learning is too narrow to capture this. "Our kids are judged by what they do on paper even though we as teachers know that's only a small percentage of what we see through the day," Kelly notes. Most teachers can't integrate garden-based teaching by themselves. They need curriculum that allows for experiential learning, time to plan and implement it, and an assessment of their students' achievements that captures and counts the broad outcomes that result from the learning garden. All of these help make garden-based learning a viable strategy for teachers.

CHALLENGES IN THE PHYSICAL GARDEN

Finally, there is the challenge of the actual, physical space of the school garden. Whatever features a garden has and no matter its size, school gardens that really work for teachers need to be designed and planted to align with schools' goals and curriculum, as well as be designed appropriately to the surroundings. Learning gardens need to support the subject content and skills that teachers have to teach; they should include habitat areas to attract pollinators and offer opportunities for observation, edible garden beds to illustrate the full cycle of plant development, and digging areas to help students discover life in the soil. Flourishing school gardens that are integrated into teachers' practice reflect the plants in their particular region, whether that means drought-tolerant or mildew-resistant. They accommodate the physical environment of the neighborhood (urban, suburban, or rural) and the social environment of the school community (such as active afterschool and summer use, or a "fallow" period through summer vacation). Learning gardens in Texas, for example, need to incorporate shaded spaces for students to gather and work; urban learning gardens might have storage "cages" where the contents are completely visible (as opposed to storage sheds) to discourage vandalism motivated by curiosity; and all school gardens should provide spaces appropriate for the school community—and sometimes the neighborhood too—to gather. In other words, successful and well-used school gardens follow design principles that allow for the enormous variety in school and neighborhood communities.

However, even well-designed gardens require maintenance. Edible gardens require constant attention during the growing season: preparing beds for planting, daily watering of seeds and small sprouts, weeding beds of annual vegetables, and harvesting. While many teachers want their students to be part of such elemental activities, few consistently have the time in their school day for the care that a garden requires to flourish.

LACK OF SUPPORT STAFF

Teachers who are depending on the learning garden for experiences upon which they can build standards-based lessons count on more than maintenance: they also need ready access to materials and supplies; garden expertise when, say, a colony of aphids settles into the cruciferous bed; and coordination between their garden plans and those of the other active garden-using teachers in the school. Given the time constraints teachers already face and the demands of the garden, it is unrealistic to assume that most public school teachers by themselves can develop, maintain, and coordinate use of their gardens. In line with other school resources that support curriculum, such as the computer lab and the school library, school gardens need support staff. Teachers consistently cite the need for support staff as a challenge even when the teacher is comfortable teaching in the garden.[4]

*   *   *   *

In spite of the large numbers of teachers convinced that the school garden can and should be part of teaching standards-based curriculum, the challenges that experienced garden-using teachers bring up over and over again are often beyond their control. They point to a lack of systematic support at the district, state, regional, or even national level. For children to access the critical experiences the learning garden provides—beyond the fortunate number who are part of a school with inspired leadership, a teacher able and willing to go the extra mile, or parents with the time and resources to keep a school garden viable—a systematic change is required.

Districtwide school garden programs are one solution that is being adopted by pioneering organizations concerned with making garden-based learning more widely available to public school students.

Districtwide garden integration allows for a bigger and more diverse community of practice among teachers. Sharing strategies, refining best practices, and unifying around challenges are all activities that encourage teachers to use their school garden more, and more deeply. That in turn means that more children are getting access to a rich garden experience in school. When integration of garden-based learning is happening at a district level, then experienced garden-using teachers can expect to keep their practice going when they move to new schools. It also means that the students those teachers leave behind won't lose their access to the learning garden if all or most remaining teachers in the school are also using the school garden.

The list of what it takes to effectively support a district's worth of teachers' practice and to more fully ground garden-based learning in public education is the starting point for the next chapters. There is work already being done that can help shape a systematic approach, one that deals head-on with the recurring challenges teachers name: the physical garden design and its ongoing maintenance, standards-based curriculum that supports experiential learning, districts and principals who confirm the value of garden-based learning for children, and, not least, time for teachers to learn outdoor teaching strategies and implement them.

A systematic approach also addresses the list of questions that leadership asks at the school and district level: how the school garden will be maintained and developed, how to sustain the commitment to garden-based professional development for teachers in the face of competing initiatives and requirements, how to clarify the role of support staff so that it is aligned with district priorities and goals, and where the funding for all of this will come from.

The pursuit of systematic best practices in garden-based learning is not new.[5] In the five stories presented in the next chapter, we will start to see the patterns, challenges, and successes that will lead to deeper garden use in schools.

CHAPTER 4

Five Models for Garden-Based Learning

A "scalable" system of garden-based learning for the whole country may not exist yet, but elements of it do. This chapter tells the story of five school districts that have invested in school gardens at a significant level to bring garden-based learning to their students. Some began through a partnership with an outside organization (such as a school garden service provider); others initiated a program within their public school system. Taken together, the following five school garden programs represent a spectrum of size and features, all serving diverse student populations with significant numbers of low-income families and English language learners.

- In the early 1990s, the City of Boston and a group of private funders forged a public/private partnership, which lasted nearly two decades, to create outdoor classrooms and train elementary teachers in outdoor science and writing in many of the city's elementary schools. While it closed its doors in 2013, the Boston Schoolyard Initiative still stands as a singular example of a city's investment in garden-based learning.
- In north Texas, six public school districts are working in partnership with a community organization to take science instruction outside to the schoolyard in nearly one hundred elementary schools.
- Cambridge Public Schools in Massachusetts is in its second decade of integrating garden-based learning throughout the district's sixteen elementary and middle schools.
- San Francisco has built an unprecedented number of learning gardens in its public schoolyards and is working with a community partner organization to integrate them in elementary science instruction.

- Most recently, Washington, DC, has launched a school garden program within the Office of the State Superintendent of Education (OSSE) as part of the DC Healthy Schools Act of 2010.

Each of these five programs has responded to a similar problem in its own manner, yet all share a vision to develop garden-based learning as a practice for teachers—through training, adoption of garden-based strategies in their standards-based curriculum, and professional development for teachers covering how to implement these new strategies. They have a similar scope in that all operate in a significant percentage of the schools in the district. Each is working on bridging edible and health outcomes with academic outcomes. There are differences, too, most obviously in demographics and geography. They also reflect a variety of approaches to the same end, but they all include some element of institutionalized funding for the program—a public commitment to support garden-based learning for all children's education. Taken together, they can tell us a lot about what integrated garden-based education can look like and what it takes to succeed.

BOSTON SCHOOLYARD INITIATIVE
Boston, Massachusetts

The Boston Schoolyard Initiative (BSI) began in 1995 as a partnership between community groups, Mayor Thomas Menino's office, and a funding collective intent on upgrading the city's public school playgrounds and schoolyards for children's play and learning. Over the course of twenty years until BSI closed its doors in 2013, BSI renovated eighty-eight urban schoolyards through a process of school and neighborhood input with professional planners and designers. In 2007, it expanded its renovations to include "outdoor classrooms," learning gardens with native plants and natural features like boulders and tree stumps, and often including raised beds for growing vegetables. They were designed for teachers to use for instruction, most frequently science instruction, outside in the schoolyard. In 2013, the Boston Schoolyard Initiative formally ended when Mayor Menino, its major champion, left office. At that point, BSI had created thirty-three learning gardens throughout Boston's public schools.

FIGURE 4.1   Outdoor classroom at Mather Elementary School, Boston Public Schools

Source: CitySprouts

History

The idea behind BSI originated in 1994, when two community groups approached Mayor Menino about the dire shortage of green space in the city's neighborhoods. Mayor Menino responded by convening the School-yard Task Force to explore possible answers to the grim situation. The result was a remarkable partnership between the Boston Public Schools district, the City of Boston, and a collective of private funders united by their vision of transformed play and learning spaces for children in Boston neighborhoods. The funding for this historical initiative represented private and community support, and focused on the potential not only to improve schools and neighborhoods but also to bridge them through a design process that actively engaged both groups of stakeholders.

Funding

The City had a grand vision for outdoor education, and its investment in it was significant. In 2008, for example, the annual capital investment from the City was $1.2 million, with a $600,000 annual investment of private dollars from the Boston Funders Collaborative and an additional $450,000 annually from the city budget to support BSI operations and professional development for teachers. The overall result was 130 acres of asphalt reclaimed as schoolyard playgrounds and outdoor classrooms.

Design

BSI approached the schoolyard as both a school resource and a neighborhood resource; therefore, community input shaped the design of BSI outdoor classrooms and playgrounds from the very beginning of the process. Students were surveyed and invited to draw maps of what they liked about their schoolyard play and learning spaces, and what they'd like to see in the new playground or outdoor classroom. Teachers were surveyed on how they currently used the schoolyard for teaching and asked to consider how it could better support them. Neighbors were asked to share their ideas for how the new outdoor classrooms could best serve the children in their neighborhood both during and outside school hours. For each project, BSI convened a volunteer school and neighborhood committee, the "Participating Schoolyard Friends Group," to represent input from their respective groups as well as to communicate back project goals and progress to them. This committee contributed to the design that the landscape architect and project manager carried forward to the installation phase. The entire process—from the time the application for a BSI schoolyard "makeover" was made available to schools until the completion of the playground and outdoor classroom installation—took two years.

Ross Miller, a design consultant who worked with BSI over many years, recalls just how much the community was invited to participate in each schoolyard design:

> The focus of schoolyard design with the landscape architect took place between the start of the new school year in September until a January presentation of drawings for the school facilities department to review . . . During this intensive five-month development, the committee of school and community members was expected to attend each monthly meeting, and to be responsible for meeting notes that are distributed in print, held

in a binder kept at the school principal's office, and shared on the Web. A design progress bulletin board was set up near the front of each school building to share drawings and monthly updates. BSI organizers insisted that the school inform the neighborhood of the design process with door-to-door flyers, by maintaining a newsletter or a Web blog, and to share design planning with the community during open houses, barbecues, and other school events.[1]

At the end of the five-month community process, the landscape architect made final adjustments and prepared plans for the bidding process required by the city. Construction was planned for June through August so that the schoolyard was ready for the beginning of the new school year.

Over eighteen years, BSI developed design principles for urban outdoor classrooms that emerged from this intensive community process. BSI educators and landscapers watched and noted the kinds of activities teachers had their students do in the schoolyard: sifting soil and pouring water, collecting samples of rocks and soil types, observing and drawing, taking notes, counting, measuring and collecting data, listening, and writing. These observations shaped the vision of the outdoor classroom as an "interactive place of discovery" that could accommodate year-round activity for full classes as well as small groups. Common features included a perimeter fence and formal entrance to the outdoor classroom, which served to define what happened *in* the learning space for students and teachers as well as what activities stayed outside (neighborhood dog walking, for example). Outdoor classrooms ideally had a gathering area for the whole class; five hundred square feet or more for an "urban meadow" of flowering perennials and a variety of grasses; a sample woodland; a work area with an "armature" to support teaching tools; individual and small group seating, such as boulders, stumps, or low stone walls; and pathways connecting all of these different spaces within the outdoor classroom.

As more and more teachers expressed the desire for garden beds in the outdoor classrooms, BSI began adding planting beds for edible gardens, too. Although edible gardens had been part of BSI's concept when it started in the mid-1990s, these had been intended less for teachers—

FIGURE 4.2   Trotter outdoor classroom site plan

Source: Courtesy of Ross Miller

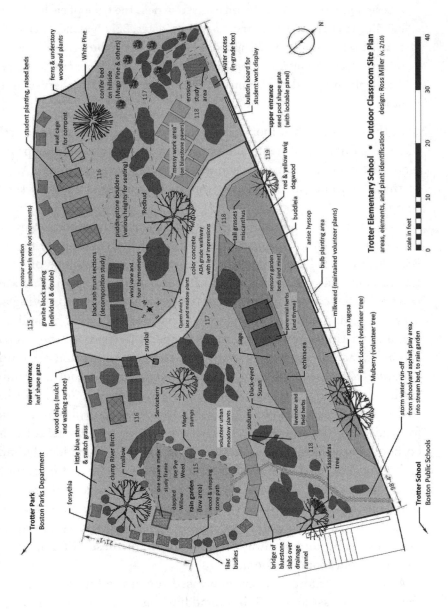

who often didn't have the means to maintain them through the summer season—than for community gardeners in the neighborhood. Initially, BSI imagined that community gardeners and teachers would find ways to garden in these spaces together. Kristin Metz, BSI's education director from 2000 to 2013, remembers the challenges of edible gardening in the early days of BSI. "There were bits and pieces . . . if you had a teacher that was an avid gardener, they could use it in wonderful ways. The problem was when the teacher left." BSI's solution was to focus on plant diversity—specifically, Kristin noted, on plant communities "that could survive whether or not someone was watering it."[2]

Support

As the inaugural education director, Kristin was charged with developing support for teachers to integrate the outdoor classrooms more fully into their curriculum. This effort had two components, both embedded in collaboration with Boston Public Schools: curriculum material for outdoor learning and professional development for teachers. The goals were to increase student engagement and academic achievement on the one hand, and to increase teachers' capacity for ongoing outdoor instruction on the other.

BSI also collaborated with two Boston Public School departments to develop teaching material for Boston's outdoor classrooms. The Outdoor Writers Workshop, started in 2008, was designed to support the district's workshop model for writing instruction. The BSI garden design, with stumps and boulders for children to perch on and nooks that gave them a relative sense of privacy, encouraged children to write.

BSI's collaboration with the district's science department, however, was the first area Kristin approached and proved to be rich fodder for BSI's vision. When the collaboration began, the district had just adopted a new curriculum and was open to exploring nontraditional settings for implementing new core ideas and practices. The science department had a robust teacher training program, including "teacher leaders" to help implement the new curriculum and foster best practices in science instruction among their colleagues. To this, BSI contributed *Science in the*

Schoolyard, a program that was entirely interwoven with the district's curriculum and the science department's own professional development.

BSI developed outdoor extensions to eighteen modules that included lesson plans as well as guidance for teachers in organizing and managing a class outdoors in the schoolyard. First graders observed air and weather in a "weather walk"; in a second-grade module, students searched for insects in the schoolyard; and fifth graders practiced using simple machines like pulleys and levers set up in the schoolyard.

BSI teacher training used the district's own science curriculum, and incorporated teaching strategies that combined outdoor, hands-on learning with the learning goals explicit in the existing curriculum. BSI workshops for teachers covered strategies for structuring outdoor lessons, fostering students' science skills (such as inquiry and observation), and managing a class of up to thirty students in the outdoor classroom. BSI developed five professional development courses for Boston teachers; over the course of *Science in the Schoolyard,* more than six hundred teachers took at least one of them. Twelve of BSI's outdoor science modules were adopted by FOSS (Full Option Science System), a national research-based science curriculum based on the principles of active learning and investigation. BSI lessons will remain available as an open source on the BSI Web site until 2018 as well as on the FOSS Web site.

Assessment

In the 2012–2013 school year, after nearly eight years of working to integrate outdoor science instruction in Boston elementary and middle schools, BSI commissioned an outside evaluation of the state of outdoor science instruction in the district. The evaluation examined the impact outdoor science lessons had on both student and teacher outcomes. It asked teachers what motivated them to make science instruction part of their practice, and how outdoor science lessons changed their practice. It also sought feedback from teachers and students on how learning science in the schoolyard changed students' attitudes about science and learning. Data was gathered from about one hundred science specialist teachers in surveys, interviews, focus groups, and direct observation. More than half of these teachers had taken one or more *Science in the Schoolyard* training classes, and about a third of the teachers came from schools with a BSI outdoor classroom. Student questionnaires were completed by 770 third through fifth graders from seven schools in the district. About half of these students came from schools with a BSI outdoor classroom.

Findings from the study revealed that students who reported going outside for science lessons with their teachers were more likely to describe science as something they liked and also something they felt confident they did well. Not all teachers had participated in BSI training, but those who had done so reported taking students outside for science more frequently than those who hadn't, even if they didn't have a BSI outdoor classroom at their school. These teachers were also more confident in their ability to teach outdoors and significantly more committed to the benefits of outdoor education for their students than teachers who had not participated in the training.

Postscript

BSI officially closed its doors at the end of 2013 after eighteen years of designing and building schoolyard playgrounds and outdoor classrooms in Boston. It was a pioneering effort that broadened not only the boundaries of outdoor classroom design but also the possibilities of collaborating with public schools at the district level to develop training for teachers, not to mention enhancing a national elementary science curriculum with practical, outdoor applications. The thirty-three BSI outdoor classrooms are an inspiring outcome from that initial frustration with the lack of public natural areas for children in Boston neighborhoods. The story of BSI illustrates how potent schoolyard learning gardens can be not only for neighborhoods but also for the work of schools. Over nearly two decades, BSI increasingly became intertwined in the workings of the public schools as it learned that it's not enough to *build* the garden— even with intensive community input in design—but teachers must be trained to *use* it, and curriculum connections in teachers' standards-based lessons (in this case, science) are as important as the physical, outdoor classroom in teachers' ability to use the space in an ongoing way. In its nearly two-decade run, BSI contributed significantly to learning garden design in urban neighborhoods as well as to the understanding of what it takes to support teachers in their ability to really use the garden.

REAL SCHOOL GARDENS

North Texas

Farther south, another organization has partnered with nearly one hundred elementary schools in six North Texas school districts to create learning gardens and train teachers in garden-based learning. REAL School Gardens—a nonprofit formed, like BSI, in the mid-1990s—builds learning gardens in low-income elementary schools and provides schools with three years of support to improve students' academic outcomes. In 2014, REAL School Gardens started a three-year partnership with a charter school in Washington, DC, beginning an expansion to a new region of the country.

History

REAL School Gardens (RSG) grew out of a project started by Texas-based philanthropist Richard Rainwater and his friend Suzy Rall Peacock in Fort Worth, Texas, in the 1990s. Beginning in 1995 with a series of learning gardens built in two schools, the project aspired to make a significant difference in the lives of children by working with public schools to connect children to the natural environment. A small group of teachers bound by an interest in garden-based learning had already been meeting annually at environmental conferences in North Texas. In 2003, Suzy Peacock began another phase of this effort by working with this group of teachers and a small support staff to explore what was needed to make school gardens sustainable and integrated into the schools where they were situated.

In 2007, this effort shifted again when Rainwater and Peacock established REAL School Gardens as a nonprofit entity with the mission to get kids excited about science, math, and language arts lessons, helping them learn the skills they needed to achieve long-term results through hands-on outdoor learning. Funded by the Rainwater Charitable Foundation and under the leadership of Executive Director Jeanne McCarty, REAL School Gardens began to scale up the program elements that Suzy and the teachers had established: garden design and installation, teacher engagement and training, and garden-based lessons that reflected the curriculum teachers used in their schools. Jeanne and her staff expanded on these early efforts by developing systems to integrate the neighborhood

FIGURE 4.3   Learning garden at Academy at C. F. Thomas Elementary, Birdville Independent School District

Source: REAL School Gardens

and business community in designing and building school gardens—involving families and neighbors as well as corporate funders and volunteers in creating teaching gardens in these cities' schools. Since 2007, the organization has expanded to over one hundred school partnerships encompassing six school districts in the Dallas-Fort Worth area.

Design

The RSG process begins when a school is selected as a partner and the organization has identified funders committed to a three-year collaboration with the school. It can look like this: in the first days of the school year, students learn that their school is "getting a garden." Within a couple of weeks, RSG organizes a schoolwide contest for students to submit their own ideas for design. A couple of weeks later, in mid-September, the school and RSG co-host a "Design & Dine" event for the next phase of the garden—community input from families, teachers, neighbors, and the funders. Students' ideas are shared, discussed, and augmented to ensure that the school's learning goals are reflected in the final design. Before the end of the first month of school, everyone is invited back for the "Big Dig," where as many as three hundred volunteers descend on the schoolyard to install the new school garden—performing tasks like building beds and planting—all in one day.

REAL School Gardens brings its own list of requirements to these new school gardens. These include *Design* features such as an enclosure (a fence or plantings) to define the learning garden area with an "evident and welcoming" entrance, a balance of deciduous and evergreen plantings, and a shade area (which might be existing large trees or a new shade arbor if there are no trees already on site). Requirements also include *Teaching & Learning* features such as plantings with historical or environmental significance (e.g., native trees and shrubs), a gathering area with a whiteboard for teacher use, a digging area for students, intentional small animal habitats (such as logs and stones to nurture insect life), and clear labels everywhere identifying plants. RSG's third design requirement is *Maintenance & Sustainability*, which covers things like easy access to water and tools, rainwater catchment systems, and a scope to the whole garden design that is reasonable to maintain.

Some features in the REAL School Gardens design actually function as both a Teaching & Learning feature as well as a Maintenance & Sustainability feature. Drip irrigation, for instance, can keep a learning garden alive in the hot Texas climate; installing it (and referring to it as an environmental practice) works as a valuable Teaching & Learning tool. "With the increased population in Texas, the demand for water has soared and we need to be reminded to respect the available water captured underground and in lakes and utilize it in a practical and useful way," garden educator Eric Vanderbeck wrote on the RSG blog.[3] "Volunteers and teachers that come to the school garden installs receive valuable training in drip irrigation techniques and are able to bring this information and application to their own home landscapes and gardens . . . there [are] on average 250 volunteers per garden installation and that means upwards of 2,500 people have been exposed to the drip irrigation watering approach. Additionally, the 10 schools conservatively have 450 students each and this shows 4,500 students the value and simple technology of water conservation."

FIGURE 4.4   Edwin J. Kiest Elementary School learning garden site plan

Source: REAL School Gardens

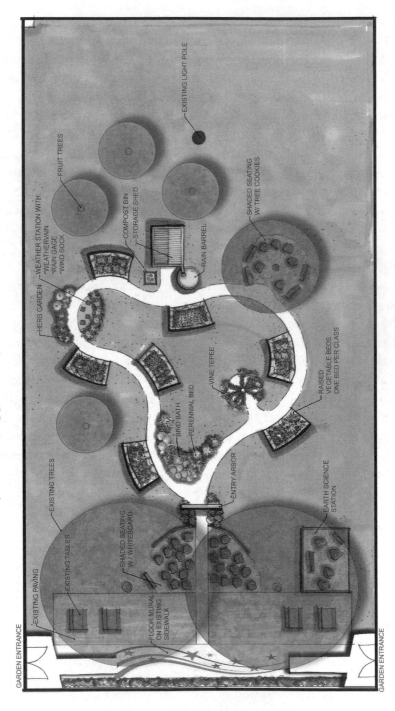

Organizing and coordinating the community to help install new school learning gardens, from soliciting community input to recruiting in-kind donors for professional services beyond the capability of the volunteers for the build, represents a significant investment for REAL School Gardens. Depending on the particular learning garden design, RSG staff might find local professionals to install ADA-compliant concrete pathways, a pond with an electric pump and flagstone "shore," or precut lumber for the raised garden beds. All is in place for the day the volunteers arrive to construct picnic tables and assemble the raised beds, install rain barrels and drip irrigation systems, paint murals, fill and plant beds, and set up small animal habitats with stumps, logs, and flat stones.

Funding

REAL School Gardens secures funding partners to cover the lion's share of the three-year program costs (around 80 percent) up front. Corporate funders receive an invitation to send their employees to the Big Dig event as volunteers. Low-income schools cover approximately 20 percent of the three-year RSG program costs. Schools that do not meet RSG's criteria for "low-income" may still participate in the program with fees adjusted upward on a sliding scale. After the initial three-year program ends, RSG offers an opportunity to extend training support to its teachers through its Evergreen Program. Schools can opt to receive continued training, garden coordinator stipends, seasonal supplies, and gardening expertise for about half of the yearly cost of their initial program fee.

Support

Once the garden is built, REAL School Gardens begins three years of training for the school's teachers on how to make the garden part of their teaching. The process starts with RSG educators developing lesson plans focused on specific standards identified by the school—for instance, life cycles or forms of energy, or math concepts like estimation or area and perimeter. This initial, all-day, all-staff training serves to introduce teachers to the new learning garden, to the program, and to the basics of outdoor education. Over the next three years, a smaller subgroup of teachers elects to receive customized one-on-one trainings with RSG

educators, all of whom have both classroom teaching experience and extensive horticulture training themselves.

REAL School Gardens also provides subject-specific training for small groups of teachers, and bigger training sessions for teachers across the RSG network of schools and school districts. These latter opportunities give teachers a chance to share their best practices and discuss trends. In effect, REAL School Gardens continues that initial effort by the teachers and Suzy Peacock: building and supporting a community of practice among teachers interested and engaged in garden-based learning. Teachers are invited to participate in special projects like Smart Potatoes, a collaboration between RSG and the Botanical Research Institute of Texas, in which teachers are given lesson plans for students to grow and study potatoes. At the conclusion of the unit, the potatoes students have grown are donated to a local food pantry, linking students' learning back to the wider community.

REAL School Gardens concludes its initial three-year commitment to schools with a second all-staff training in the third and final year. This second training is intended to build on and deepen the garden-based practice teachers have developed over three years. The aim, Jeanne says, is to get 50 percent of the teachers really utilizing the garden in depth, keeping the garden in mind as they plan lessons and units of study. "That's how you really impact a school and its teaching culture," she declares.[4]

RSG's teacher support is provided by four staff educators who train teachers in the partner schools. The teacher training is supplemented by a garden coordinator in each school, a role filled by one or two of the school's teachers. RSG teacher-garden coordinators receive an annual stipend of $400 to be the school's learning garden point-person and liaison with RSG. All of the teacher-garden coordinators within a cohort (the schools that all begin a partnership with RSG at the same time) meet three times a year with RSG staff to share practices and challenges. The teacher-garden coordinators are responsible for collecting data from their school (via a teacher survey) on topics such as how many teachers are using the school garden and how they are using it. They are also in charge of distributing garden supplies (provided by RSG) to other teachers in their school.

Assessment

REAL School Gardens evaluates the success of its efforts through two outcomes: improving teacher effectiveness and increasing student engagement. It measures these factors first by documenting student access to the learning garden experience (reflected in the number of students getting garden time with their teachers), and secondly by asking teachers and other school community members about their students' sustained engagement resulting from their learning time in the school garden. The latter has shown (through an annual survey disseminated to teachers in the program, discussed next) to increase teachers' effectiveness as they integrate the skills and knowledge they gain from teaching outside. (See appendix A for examples.)

In 2010, RSG commissioned a three-year evaluation of its program to better understand the impact it was having in its partner schools. Over the course of three years, over five thousand surveys were evaluated and teachers in ten schools were interviewed. To measure how comprehensively teachers were utilizing the garden for academic instruction, teachers' survey responses were ranked on a scale from teacher's "disinterest" in using the garden for instruction to a maximum of "deepening," when a teacher reports that he or she is planning lessons with the garden in mind. Findings showed that participation in RSG teacher training beyond the initial all-school introduction was related to significant increases in teacher effectiveness as well as in student engagement in learning, both indicators of students' long-term academic success. However, only teachers who had received the training reported these outcomes, and the more training teachers participated in, the higher their gain. Teachers in schools that had a school garden but had not participated in subsequent training (after the initial all-staff orientation) did not report these outcomes. That finding confirmed how critical the teacher training is in creating a culture of school garden use.

Postscript

Beginning in the 2014–2015 school year, REAL School Gardens takes its first step toward a national program as it partners with the Yu Ying Public Charter School in Washington, DC. This new school partnership represents the first phase of an expansion of the program outside of Texas.

Supported in part by an OSSE School Gardens Program grant, REAL School Gardens joins a network of community partners in school gardening already established in the district. In DC, RSG brings a focus on science instruction and academic outcomes to a community that's been more focused on health and wellness. In Washington, DC, REAL School Gardens translates its model to a very different part of the country and the garden-based learning environment it finds there.

CITYSPROUTS
Cambridge, Massachusetts

The CitySprouts school garden program is a nonprofit organization focused on integrating garden-based learning in high-need, urban public elementary and middle schools. Partnering with twenty elementary and middle schools in Boston and Cambridge, the CitySprouts program serves a total student population of six thousand students, with 45 percent from low-income households in Cambridge and 78 percent from low-income households in Boston. CitySprouts has been working with all of the elementary and middle schools in the Cambridge Public Schools district for more than a decade to integrate garden-based learning in teachers' practice and school culture. Recognizing a need for support for garden-based learning in high-need Boston schools, CitySprouts expanded to a cluster of four Boston public schools in 2012.

History
CitySprouts started in 1999 when a few parents (myself among them), teachers, and a school principal came together with the idea of expanding garden-based learning in the city's twelve K–8 schools. The program began as a project in two schools with a couple of volunteers leading simple gardening and cooking activities in the classroom, and a handful of teachers making time in their school day for these classroom "guests." As soon as the weather allowed in the spring, the weekly garden time migrated outside, where students planted vegetable seeds in the garden beds teachers had made in the schoolyard. Joe Petner, principal of the Haggerty School at that time, describes why he signed on for the CitySprouts program: "[The garden] helped us actualize some of the ideals

FIGURE 4.5 Learning garden at Haggerty Elementary School, Cambridge Public Schools

Source: Courtesy of Laura Sewrey

we wanted to create for our school. It was not a hard sell. The strings that I attached were that it not be a one-year undertaking and that we really thought about it over time so that it would get well entrenched."[5]

Joe imagined that a school garden would soften the lines between the institutional school and the neighborhood into which it was trying to fit. Establishing a garden in the schoolyard was a way to connect with the neighborhood that was already there. It was also a way to communicate to students and families the educational approach of the Haggerty School. Joe wanted it to feel like home to the students: "In your house, you would have gardens and some space for growing things, and you would try to bring the outdoors in and the indoors out. I felt that it had to do with a school being welcoming. To not have it feel 'strict'—kids in rows, being expected to be in the same place—[and instead] much more of a developmental concept, more personal contact. That was the overarching view for me of what we were trying to create."

Between 2001 and 2008, CitySprouts expanded to the rest of the K–8 schools in Cambridge Public Schools district. Most of the CitySprouts schoolyard gardens were constructed with grassroots fundraising and volunteer labor, with parents at the school playing a major role in both areas. Not infrequently, a CitySprouts garden is built onto an existing schoolyard vegetable or flower garden that was created by teachers or parents. CitySprouts early edible learning gardens expanded and developed in response to teachers' requests and as fundraising allowed. Most were begun with no more than a few thousand dollars, which paid for four or five raised beds and soil to fill them, a tool shed, a compost bin, seeds, and plants.

Design
The CitySprouts garden design and installation process has become more predictable as the organization has grown and its partnership with Cambridge Public Schools has matured, although new CitySprouts gardens are still budgeted under $10,000 and rely extensively on parent and community labor. Recently, however, CitySprouts has been invited to contribute school garden design expertise to the city as school building renovations are planned. The City of Cambridge, for its part, has increasingly undertaken learning garden construction or maintenance projects that are funded in the city budget rather than dependent on parent fundraising, and carried out by the Department of Public Works instead of volunteers. Learning garden maintenance is shared by CitySprouts and the Cambridge Public Schools facilities department; principals' requests for learning garden upgrades or repairs are more frequently rolled into the school department's overall facility plan.

Support
The goal of CitySprouts is to make a change in children's learning and health (that is, increasing students' engagement in learning, developing their understanding of the natural world, and improving their food choices) and in teachers' capacity to sustain garden-based learning as an element of their teaching practice. While CitySprouts' service to its partner schools includes building and developing edible learning gardens in the schoolyard as needed (and occasionally within community gardens

nearby), the program devotes the majority of its resources, funneled through the CitySprouts garden coordinator, to supporting teachers' garden activity. Each garden coordinator is responsible for the school community and his or her learning garden at a cluster of four schools. For some teachers, "garden activity" might be one lesson in the fall for science observation and then a spring visit to help plant the gardens. For other teachers, it means monthly or even weekly visits to the garden for lessons in science, writing, math, or social studies. A necessary part of supporting teachers' garden use is overseeing maintenance of the garden as a teaching environment. Making the garden accessible to teachers includes ensuring that it's planted and cared for—in other words, that it is organized and thriving.

At the insistence of the teachers and principal in the group, there was from the start a strong focus on documenting how teachers incorporated CitySprouts' early classroom and garden activities into larger learning goals. One benefit of this practice has been to see how teachers' approach to CitySprouts and the school garden has changed over time. Teachers' garden use has been a primary force in shaping how CitySprouts has developed over the years as teachers increasingly planned how their students' garden experience would support, enhance, or highlight core concepts taught throughout the year. Over the years, more and more teachers have incorporated CitySprouts' annual cider pressing activity into writing lessons, math word problems, or a simple machines component in the fifth-grade science unit. In effect, CitySprouts' cider pressing has evolved from a seasonal food activity to a springboard for teachers' lessons back in the classroom.

Funding

From the very beginning, school principals were asked to contribute funds to the program in their school. The CitySprouts contract outlined the services it would provide to the school: to develop and maintain an edible learning garden on school grounds, to provide support to teachers to develop garden-based lessons and utilize the learning garden for instruction, to support school and district health and learning initiatives (such as cafeteria healthy food campaigns and afterschool garden clubs), and as of 2009, to provide a summer internship for middle school youth in the school garden during the summer. The initial cost to schools was $1,500. When CitySprouts became a districtwide program in 2006, funding for CitySprouts was added as a line item to the annual school budget through the science department and formalized CitySprouts' agreement with Cambridge Public Schools to support teachers within the district's standards-based curriculum. Currently, Cambridge Public Schools funds one-third of the operating cost of the program in the city, and the remaining two-thirds comes from foundation grants and private donations.

In 2007, the science department approached CitySprouts about working together to create garden-based extensions to the district's science curriculum. The end product was *Curriculum Connections*, a document that outlined garden activities or projects that extended or deepened science units at each grade from kindergarten through eighth grade. (See an example in appendix B.) Second-grade teachers teaching the soil unit, for instance, are given directions that outline steps to make a trip to the garden as part of the scope and sequence of the unit. These steps might include a visit to the garden to look under a rotting log (or stepping stones) for insect life. Sixth-grade classes comparing different root systems might work with the garden coordinator to pull up a variety of plants to examine their roots, and while they're in the garden, to set traps for isopods (pill bugs). *Curriculum Connections* is a means for the district science educators to inform teachers about what garden activities are possible, how they fit in the curriculum's scope and sequence, and how the CitySprouts garden coordinator can help support the lesson.

The following year, in 2008, Cambridge Public Schools science educators and CitySprouts collaborated on professional development, known as *Science in the Garden*, that was implemented at four of the district's twelve K–8 schools to explain key topics in the science curriculum and give teachers a grounding in using the school gardens and the CitySprouts program for teaching science. The results were captured in an evaluation that confirmed that this sample of teachers did indeed find that *Curriculum Connections* and the accompanying training helped them expand their use of the garden for science instruction. Among the findings, teachers viewed the gardens as providing a learning experience that helped students understand science concepts more deeply and fully. Teachers were uniform in their belief that students were more engaged in learning when taught in garden-based lessons compared to lessons taught solely in the classroom. In addition, the *Science in the Garden* training, in conjunction with other science department activities to support garden-based lessons, appeared to slightly increase teachers' use of the garden for science instruction.[6]

Lisa Scolaro, then curriculum coordinator for science in Cambridge Public Schools and now its acting director of science, technology, engineering, and math, explains what motivated her team to make a place for garden-based learning in the city's elementary schools. "We wanted teachers to use the space [the learning gardens] and take what they already had to do and make it more meaningful or more real-world for students. We didn't think that every teacher had the time to go through and think, 'Oh, this would work well in the garden, and this wouldn't work well in the garden.' If we did that for teachers, we thought, it might get used more, and it would get used in support of our units while supporting the garden at the same time. It sends the message that we both value this: that [CitySprouts] values our curriculum, and that we value the [garden] space, too."[7]

Assessment

CitySprouts looks for four outcomes from its program: an increase in children's academic engagement, children making healthier food choices, children demonstrating understanding and appreciation of the natural world, and an increased capacity for teachers to sustain garden-based learning as a practice. Like the other programs described in this book, CitySprouts is committed to creating a system that serves the needs of children with fewer resources—low-income students, English language learners, and children who struggle to achieve academic proficiency. CitySprouts measures its progress through an annual survey to teachers in its partner schools in June and through a pre- and post-survey to the one hundred middle school youth participating in the CitySprouts summer program each year. (See appendix A.) Additionally, in 2010 CitySprouts underwent a program evaluation to capture the impact of the *Science in the Garden* collaboration with the Cambridge Public Schools science department.

Results from CitySprouts' 2014 annual survey to teachers show that more than 80 percent of teachers in Cambridge and 55 percent of teachers in Boston consistently utilize their learning garden for instruction. The return rate on the CitySprouts survey has been between 95 and 100 percent since the organization started collecting this information from teachers in 2006 (until 2012, teachers completed two surveys in the school year, one in late November and the other in June). The 2010 evaluation, conducted by consultant Neil Schiavo, included data from these surveys (as a baseline and post-workshops) as well as interviews with eight teachers who participated in the science workshops and Cambridge Public Schools' science department staff. Findings from the evaluation showed a slight increase in participating teachers' garden use, and affirmed that teachers perceived that the learning gardens "helped students understand science concepts more deeply and fully."[8]

Postscript

In addition to its efforts during the school year, CitySprouts has addressed the issue of summer garden use by creating a summer program for middle school youth in grades six through eight, a group whose teachers use the learning garden significantly less than do elementary teachers. In the monthlong internship in July and August, more than one hundred young people learn about garden ecosystems and the practical skills of cooking with fresh produce. The program is supported in part by the City of Cambridge and has a strong working relationship with the City's own youth program. In 2011, CitySprouts became a service site for FoodCorps, an AmeriCorps initiative to establish food education and healthy food access in high-need schools and communities. The three FoodCorps members serving their year with CitySprouts focus on food education in school and after school in CitySprouts' partner schools in Cambridge and Boston.

CitySprouts illustrates an emerging relationship between a school district open to a new idea, and a tenacious community group of parents, classroom teachers, science educators, and principals fueled by teachers' interest and children's enthusiasm. CitySprouts' partnership with Cambridge Public Schools is a reflection of the work of a decade of garden co-ordinators exploring with hundreds of teachers what integrated garden-based learning looks like from the ground up.

EDUCATION OUTSIDE
San Francisco, California

Education Outside is a nonprofit school garden program working in the San Francisco Unified School District (SFUSD) to utilize school gardens in support of science education. Education Outside evolved from a grass-roots coalition, the San Francisco Green Schoolyard Alliance, that was instrumental in securing nearly $14 million in city bond funding specifi-cally to design and construct San Francisco's public schoolyards in three distinct bond issues in 2003, 2006, and 2011. Eighty-four schoolyards were "greened" and fifty-five school gardens were created with this pub-lic funding. In the 2013–2014 school year, 59 percent of SFUSD students were low income and 27 percent were English language learners.[9] As of 2012, Education Outside has partnered with almost a third of the dis-trict's schools.

Education Outside connects schools with needed resources, provides teachers with professional development training, and makes available an open source curriculum (Lesson Pathway) that's aligned with Com-mon Core standards. Education Outside also serves as a liaison between the fifty-five schools in the district with school gardens and the SFUSD facilities department.

Design

San Francisco Bay Area schoolyards have a long history of garden-based learning compared to other parts of the country. The public schoolyards today reveal a wide variety of learning gardens that show just how much California has taken a leadership role in the evolution of school garden design and garden-based learning. A tour of SFUSD schoolyard gardens offers an invitation to consider what's possible, and the repetition of cer-tain features gives the sense that many things have been tried and prov-en true.

FIGURE 4.6   Alvarado Elementary School, San Francisco Unified School District

Source: Photo by Paige Green

Part of the wonder of the area's school gardens is due to the year-round growing season and spectacular variety of vegetation and edible plants that thrive in the Bay Area climate. The school gardens—with their abundant vegetable gardens, towering rosemary shrubs, and vast array of succulents—illustrate just how much a community can use that advantage. Garden features are imaginative, diverse, and beautiful, incorporating natural materials as varied as straw-bale construction and woven sapling trellises, waterways bordered by large boulders and grasses, and art commissioned by local artists reflecting the place-specific, deeper ecosystem surrounding the garden. Gates, totems, and informational signs establish a sense of entering a distinct place. The details in these entrances connect the garden to its surroundings in often subtle ways; the rustic wood-carved sign above the curved gate at Tule Elk Park Early Education School, for instance, is a reminder of the "nature" that underlies that particular urban neighborhood.

The wide, substantial pathways in many of San Francisco's school gardens are likewise a reminder that their construction was funded by public bond funds intended to accommodate wheelchair access. There are many whimsical details in the gardens, too, such as the "happy pig" bench at Tule Elk Park; utilitarian features, like an outdoor sink to wash garden produce; and child-centric plantings, like beanpole teepees and other kid-size spaces.

The toolsheds redefine "accessible" by not just accommodating, but actually inviting, use by both children and adults. Many of them are shallow and long so that a whole class of children can approach at the same time. Everything is visible, and reachable by small hands. The tool storage design makes it clear that school gardens are a place for children to *do* things. The gardens are thoughtfully integrated with the bigger schoolyard (including playgrounds and ball-playing spaces) and the adjacent neighborhood.

There is a resourceful integration of environmental practices reflected in the learning gardens in California, as indicated by the frequency of three-bin composting in urban schoolyards to show the distinct stages of decomposition, or the ubiquitous solar panels to operate pumps in ponds. And in a country familiar with drought, nearly every garden has a water feature—practical ones, like irrigation and cisterns for the dry climate, but also ponds to create wildlife habitats or aqueducts that reveal water pathways from source to plant.

History

Arden Bucklin-Sporer has been active with the cities' school gardens since the early 1990s, first volunteering as a garden coordinator in her son's school, and later taking a leadership role in organizing garden coordinators at schools throughout the district. The Green Schoolyard Alliance had a small office in the SFUSD building in the facility department, where Arden wrote grants, joined the SFUSD landscape crew, and, as she

says, "tried to knit the school garden community and the city together."
She tells the story of a transformative moment in the city's long history
with public school gardens.

> [School gardens in the city] were often run by one parent, and the parent
> was there until their kid graduates and then they were moving on. Gar-
> dens were falling into disrepair . . . there were all sorts of problems. The
> big change happened in about 2002 when the school district was going
> to post another bond, [as they did] every decade or so to renovate build-
> ings, build new buildings, whatever they needed to do. And in this case
> it was doing ADA upgrade because kids [in wheelchairs] couldn't get in
> doorways, get up ramps, things like that. So a group of people who had
> formed, called the San Francisco Green Schoolyard Alliance, said, "Let's
> get some funding in that bond set aside for greening." And we did, and
> that was the beginning of this whole transformation of the school dis-
> trict. It was a tiny little slice of the bond . . . but that 1 percent translated
> into $14 million, about $150,000 per school, and it wasn't [intended] for
> anything but design and construction.
>
> So now we've had three bonds and the greening piece has been in each
> one of those bonds. I think the district had come to realize that green
> schoolyards really change the feeling of these schools. It's really a platform
> for community; it really makes the school more inviting to the public.[10]

A beginning step in creating a new schoolyard garden in SFUSD was
gathering school and neighborhood communities' input into design and
construction. Because the bond funds were solely for design and installation, however, SFUSD stipulated that each school community was expected to be active in the care and maintenance of the schoolyard project after it was built. An overview of schoolyard garden maintenance
and repair delineating responsibilities of SFUSD facilities and the school
community is outlined in a guidelines document; it includes details such
as at what point the schoolyard "reverts" to facilities and their general,
"non-schoolyard" maintenance plan.

No funding was included in the bond to support teachers in integrating and using this new resource. "That's where we really felt that
we had an opportunity," explained Arden. "Here are these fantastic,

vibrant, incredibly interesting outdoor classrooms that are just these perfect platforms for teaching elementary science. And of course we grow food, and we eat food, and we do all those kinds of things, but we do it through the lens of science. So that has ensured really deep principal buy-in, really deep teacher buy-in, and it also has given us a very clear direction."

Support

Education Outside provides its partner schools with garden-based science instructors and oversight of the school garden's care and maintenance. This service to schools is provided by Education Outside's twenty or so Corps members, each assigned for a two-year period to one of the elementary and K–8 partner schools in the district. The Corps for Education Outside was launched in 2011 as a national AmeriCorps initiative to teach science and involve the school community in caring for the outdoor learning space. The Corps is also responsible for promoting environmentally sustainable practices in schools, like energy and water conservation and composting. Corps members learn the skills and content through professional development training to continue to make an impact after the two-year service has ended. At the start of their two-year term, Corps members receive "boot camp" training in outdoor education strategies and science curriculum (such as FOSS, widely used by schools in the district) and garden curriculum aligned with science standards (such as Life Lab's classic, *The Growing Classroom*). This training prepares them to teach science to all of the students in the school at least once a week and support whatever environmental initiatives are happening inside their school, including lunchroom composting, walk/bike to school events, and reduced energy consumption.

SFUSD has developed curriculum, too, much of it in collaboration with community partners including Education Outside (and before that, the Green Schoolyard Alliance). Education Outside Corps members might use the city's Watershed Stewardship Program, an elementary-grade curriculum developed by the Public Utilities Commission. The city department, San Francisco Environment, also offers a comprehensive set of curriculum for school-age children.

Funding

Education Outside is funded through foundation, government, and corporate grants, as well as individual donors. Additionally, its public school partners pay a site fee based on a sliding scale reflecting a school's low-income population. While Education Outside's operating budget is currently funded at 30 percent federal or local sources (including a sliding-scale fee to its partner schools), its goal is to diversify to an even 25 percent from four sources: federal, private foundation, corporate and individual, and service fees from the schools it serves.

Education Outside is developing a model for supporting schools with learning gardens within the particularly rich environment of garden-based learning in California: an agricultural economy with a strong food culture, initiatives like the Green Schoolyard Alliance that grew out of many years of active parent involvement in schools, and many generations of teachers who've made garden-based learning a central part of their classroom practice. School gardening in and out of school time is already established in many parts of the state. In a 2014 survey distributed by the California School Garden Network and Life Lab, over five hundred responses confirmed schools' academic and farm-to-school garden use. Life Lab estimates that about a quarter of California's ten thousand or so schools have school gardens.[11] Education Outside is building on these efforts to establish a model for sustainable garden-based learning in San Francisco's public schools to continue this tradition equitably and sustainably.

OSSE SCHOOL GARDEN PROGRAM
Washington, DC

School gardens are blossoming in Washington, DC. Boasting ninety-three public, charter, and private schools with an active school garden and more than a dozen nonprofit organizations providing schools with school garden support, the city is in the vanguard of school garden activity. The District of Columbia has unprecedented support for school-based health initiatives from its city councilors. It is enhanced by the high-profile efforts in children's health and diet of local denizen First

Lady Michelle Obama. It also boasts the nation's first school garden program established by legislation, tax-funded, and housed in the District of Columbia Office of the State Superintendent of Education (OSSE).

History

The OSSE School Garden Program emerged in 2010 as part of a comprehensive set of initiatives for children's health called the DC Healthy Schools Act. It grew out of concern about high rates of hunger-related problems for children in the district, including obesity and healthy food access, and was intended to reach children in need through positive changes in the school environment. The DC Healthy Schools Act propelled a number of significant changes in the district. First, it addressed access to healthy food by requiring schools to participate in the federal meals program (which means making the option available to families and collecting data so that the district can collect federal reimbursement for participating students), made school breakfast universally available free of charge for all students (76 percent of whom are low-income), and eliminated families' copay for reduced-price school meals. It also raised nutrition standards in the district and established minimum levels for students' physical activity.[12] The Act also addressed environmental issues by encouraging school best practices such as schoolwide recycling, composting, and energy reduction. Lastly, it took ownership of food and nutrition education in its schools by establishing a school garden program and a farm-to-school program. In effect, this legislation catapulted the district's health and wellness policies to the top of the national list as one of the most comprehensive in the country. Washington, DC, is the only state that collects student health data from students in fifth grade, eighth grade, and high school.

Design

Given the vision of the DC Healthy Schools Act, it is not surprising that most of the district school gardens are the edible kind. But schools have created other kinds of school gardens, too—pollinator, native plant, and rain catchment gardens, for instance. Some have hoop houses large enough to walk inside, and many others have hoop-covered raised beds to extend the growing season. There are gathering areas for classes, art-

FIGURE 4.7   Learning garden at Capital City Public Charter School, Washington, DC

Source: District of Columbia Office of the State Superintendent of Education

ful entrances to outdoor classrooms, and a wide range of tool storage sheds and units. Some gardens have bees. One high school with a greenhouse grows seedlings for other elementary and middle schools in the neighborhood.

Support and Funding

Sam Ullery is the inaugural director of the OSSE School Garden Program. He is responsible for keeping track of the number of teachers using the school gardens, the number of hours students are engaged in the school gardens, and, in this developing climate, the number of new school gardens created each year. Sam oversees material resources offered through the district and coordinates the growing network of schools implementing garden-based learning. That includes "match making" between schools and the many nonprofit partners offering services and resources, overseeing the school garden grant program, assisting schools in building (or reactivating) school gardens, connecting garden coordinators and teachers to resources such as garden-based curricula, and training and providing technical assistance in utilizing the school garden. Training topics cover basic garden skills, the use of curriculum resources, and classroom management.

One of the unique features of the OSSE School Garden Program is its role in facilitating the school garden partners active in the city. For the most part these are organizations operating with funding from donations and foundation grants, and they have formed partnerships directly with individual schools. OSSE helps connect these partnerships to the resources they need to thrive by offering training for garden coordinators and teachers, providing a network for them to meet and share directly, highlighting garden-based curricula, and supplying funding to support school garden programs through a competitive grant program.

The OSSE School Garden competitive grant program provides grants of up to $15,000 to schools to "engage students and integrate nutrition themes into school curriculum." At least 80 percent of the grant must go toward support of the school garden coordinator. These schools are required to participate in a two-day intensive training for garden educators led by OSSE or one of its partners. In 2013, twenty-two schools across all eight city wards received grants (and in 2014, REAL School Gardens joins that network of school partnerships as it begins a new three-year partnership at the Yu Ying Public Charter School).

Garden coordinators' roles vary from school to school, but what they share is responsibility for three broad areas: program management of the garden (including community involvement in it), technical skills in gardening and cooking to maximize the garden's growing potential, and instruction in utilizing the garden for teachers and students. Almost half of the garden coordinators in DC schools are funded through OSSE school garden grants, moving the district closer to its goal of all schools having a garden coordinator in some capacity or another.

Assessment

A significant part of Sam's job is setting up systems for a citywide school garden program that—because it is DC—also happens to be the equivalent of a statewide system. The framework for the garden coordinator job description is one of the documents Sam created. It is part of a broader assessment meant to give feedback to both document and help develop a common tool for determining what a successful school garden program should look like. OSSE uses a rubric organized in four areas—garden design, systems, program organization, and instruction in the garden—which help to establish guidelines for the many partners. (See appendix C.) "Systems" includes natural systems like compost and irrigation as well as social systems like community participation. "Program organization" looks at sustainability supports such as funding, the role of the garden coordinator in the program, and student involvement in the garden. "Instruction" covers whether a standards-based curriculum is implemented and the variety of teaching strategies or techniques garden educators employ; this area also covers teacher involvement in the garden instruction, and the impact of the program on students' attitude and behavior in a measurable way. The data collected from schools' self-reporting and Sam's formal program observations are included in an annual report on the state of the district's school gardens.

Another element of Sam's job as director of the OSSE program is establishing citywide healthy food events, which he does in conjunction with the farm-to-school director, also a position funded by the DC Healthy Schools Act. All schools in the city are invited to participate in seasonal projects, such as the citywide Growing Healthy Schools Week, a celebration of the harvest season highlighted by taste tests and activities in the school gardens. OSSE is the DC office responsible for nominating DC schools for the federal Green Ribbon School Program, which recognizes schools across the country for improving the environmental health of schools and school practices. "Winning improvements" include reducing environmental impact and costs, improving the health and wellness of students and staff, and incorporating effective environmental education.

Postcript

The OSSE School Garden Program is taking an unusual approach for a city government: investing in the efforts of community programs to build a culture of gardens in its city's schools. Washington, DC, is actively reaching out to the privately funded organizations partnering with its schools with the goal of strengthening the school garden network with well-placed resources such as program and resource assessment, frameworks for job descriptions, professional training, and—critical-ly—grants to help these partnerships continue to grow. It represents a remarkable and comprehensive system of support for garden-based education for the city's children and youth.

*   *   *   *   *

Altogether, these five programs serve as a departure point for identifying how garden-based education can take root in the least resourced of our public schools. In spite of the geographic distance between them and the underlying variety of their approaches, the five models described here share a goal of trying to work *with* public school culture in an effort to be accessible to a great many more children than school gardens now serve. The next chapters take a closer look at where their collective experience leads.

CHAPTER 5

Lessons for Districtwide
Garden Programs

At first glance, the five garden-based education programs profiled in the previous chapter might seem to have more differences than similarities. For starters, the climates in which these gardens grow vary from hot and dry in Texas to temperate on the West Coast to the four distinct seasons of the East Coast. The school communities and neighborhoods in North Texas, San Francisco, Washington, DC, and the Boston area also represent remarkable diversity. A third point of contrast is in the very premise of the garden programs—that is, whether the garden was established as a health initiative, an academic support, or a neighborhood/schoolyard greening.

Yet these five organizations also have something very fundamental in common. They are all responding to the barriers repeatedly cited by teachers and research and outlined in chapter 3: a lack of curriculum connections to the learning garden, a need for support staff to assist in teaching outside and oversee the garden maintenance, and insufficient time in the school day for teachers to incorporate a new resource like the learning garden. As this chapter will discuss, the ways in which these organizations have approached these challenges and the patterns that emerge can show us how garden-based learning might be adopted on a large scale.

DESIGNING A GARDEN FOR ACTIVE LEARNING

The schools partnering with these five organizations can't assume that there are enough parents or teachers in their community with the time and resources to maintain their schoolyard gardens through the growing season (especially when school isn't in session). The majority of them are urban schools serving a low-income population with a majority of parents working in jobs outside the home. These are schools that can't always rely on parents having the time to maintain the school garden or coordinate its use. Many are in densely populated neighborhoods where public green space is at a premium. There's a growing body of literature about school garden design for urban neighborhoods,[1] but the best practices emerging from these five programs are less about the particular features of garden design than about the principles and processes of use—how to establish a thriving learning garden that serves the neighborhood while maximizing teachers' ability to integrate learning gardens into their classroom practice.

Putting this principle into practice begins with creating the garden, or even before, by involving teachers and students in the learning garden design process. As did the Boston Schoolyard Initiative, REAL School Gardens and Education Outside both begin their design process with children's input as well as teachers' feedback. For REAL School Gardens, this means a schoolwide call to students for design ideas, followed by its "Design & Dine" community event, where those ideas are acknowledged and considered. The Boston Schoolyard Initiative likewise elicited both student and community input before designers began to create a blueprint for a new outdoor classroom. But it doesn't stop there: these organizations invest in training teachers and garden coordinators on using the garden as an instructional space, then document how teachers use their school gardens through surveys, interviews, and focus groups.

School gardens that get a lot of teacher use are designed and planted with teachers' practice in mind—that is, with the things teachers need to help meet their students' learning goals. The list of plants and features is less important than these criteria, and in fact sometimes "cool and exciting" garden features get in the way of creating a garden that has the best possible chance of integrating with teachers' curriculum and school culture. The stories in this book illustrate that learning gardens that work for teachers can also be active for community and afterschool and food education, but not all active school gardens also work for teachers. Ensuring that gardens are designed with teachers' instruction in mind is the foundation for strong teacher garden use.

Bridging the Gap to Families and Neighborhood

Effective learning garden design also needs to connect the school with families and neighbors. Former Cambridge school principal Joe Petner notes the role that the garden played in lowering the barrier between what families and neighbors might see as the "institution" represented by the school building and the more organic, social nature of the neighborhood.

At Education Outside, inviting the community to be part of the process from the initial design to the actual installation of the learning garden is a key organizing principle, just as it was for the Boston Schoolyard Initiative. Imagining and creating the schoolyard garden together helps to establish right from the start that the outdoor space belongs to both the school and the neighborhood and can serve as a conduit between them. Sam Ullery at the OSSE School Garden Program noticed how much his city's school gardens seemed to invite families to be part of the school community. He emphasizes how much Washington, DC, school gardens are used for community gathering: "[The school garden] has special characteristics of being both a community space but also a *living* space. It sets the tone for the school and its culture."[2]

Learning gardens also need to include vegetable beds as a way to promote nutrition education and foster connections between the school and the families who live nearby. Increasingly, schools are expected to play a role in health and wellness, and the learning garden is a natural venue for making that happen effectively. Since 2006, any school participating in the National School Lunch Program is required to create a Local Wellness Policy with the intention to increase opportunities for healthy eating and physical activity. Even as the five programs in this book drive home the fact that most schools don't have dedicated time in the school day for nutrition education, having an edible learning garden on site opens up the possibility that nutrition and food education can be part of children's school experience.

More explicitly, edible learning gardens establish connections between children's experience in the schoolyard garden and food served at lunch, helping them make healthier food choices in and out of school and supporting families' healthy eating efforts at home. The OSSE School Garden Program, which emerged from a healthy food and nutrition initiative, is the most obvious example of this, but all five programs illustrate schools' attempts to establish the connection between growing food in the schoolyard and making healthy food choices. Both OSSE and CitySprouts are partners in the national FoodCorps program.

Ensuring Access for All

Another design principle reflected in all five organizations is access, or considering how the garden space welcomes all kinds of learners, no matter their physical or intellectual differences. San Francisco's school garden design actually developed in response to funding specifically for ADA compliance, but all five of the programs profiled in this book have absorbed the principle of access—for example, by designing paths to accommodate wheelchairs and considering how the garden will serve English language learners. Even maintaining clear signage and access to the tool and supply shed can be considered an access issue in that it facilitates teachers' ability to approach the garden on their own, when they can. In short, these five organizations have all embraced a definition of access as a schoolyard learning garden that is approachable, sustainable, and practical so that the highest possible number of children are served by it.

These gardens are designed to ensure access by also giving urban children an experience of nature that they may not otherwise get. The gardens have edible beds that engage students in the activities of the seasons: digging, planting, watering, and harvesting. No matter the climate, the rhythms of a vegetable garden physically engage children in predictable ways each season, and at the same time introduce new, unpredictable opportunities and challenges inherent in growing things. The gardens also have natural habitat areas where students observe nature in uncultivated spaces. Like the edible garden beds, the natural habitat areas reflect the particular climate of the place, its own flora and fauna.

These learning gardens are often designed to connect what's happening in the schoolyard with environmental practices inside the school. San Francisco's schoolyard gardens are a good example of how the learning garden intentionally mirrors the environmental practices inside the building, like composting, conserving water, and appreciating local food production systems.

"Everything you do in the outdoor classroom is also environmental education," says Education Outside Director Arden Bucklin-Sporer. "Understanding systems, understanding how this small little outdoor classroom might fit into a larger context like the nearby natural areas, how we best promote biodiversity and conserve our natural resources. There's no doubt that environmental literacy is layered on [outdoor science education]." The learning gardens are one more way that children are connected to their larger community, and they explicitly support children's understanding of systems thinking.

GARDEN MAINTENANCE AND SUPPORT STAFF: KEEPING THE GARDEN GROWING

The five case studies also illustrate ways to address challenges related to support staff and garden maintenance when school isn't in session. CitySprouts staff and the Education Outside Corps fold in summer garden maintenance as part of their service to their partner schools, while REAL School Gardens and the OSSE School Garden Program require that their partner schools create a maintenance plan (which REAL School Gardens supplements by coordinating volunteers from local Master Gardeners programs). The Boston Schoolyard Initiative addressed the issue of maintenance first by incorporating low-maintenance plantings in its design and then advocating for a school-department-funded maintenance oversight position. All five programs have employed design, process, and program as strategies to address the perennial issue of maintenance.

The Garden Coordinator

Education Outside's and CitySprouts' school-based support staff (and the garden coordinators that OSSE funds) help to coordinate the garden maintenance plan, but a much bigger part of their job is focused on children's access to the garden either directly or through their classroom teacher. They are, as Arden frames it, " . . . the person to rally the troops, bring teachers to trainings, get the outdoor classroom ready for classes, be a real partner to the teachers."

Teachers often need assistance for even well-planned activities in the garden. Not unlike in the computer lab or even the school library, teaching in the school garden is enhanced with a technical "expert": Education Outside has established its Corps, OSSE oversees and trains garden coordinators from a dozen partner organizations, and REAL School Gardens trains and stipends teachers for this task. Although these are different models for support staff, they share a few responsibilities: serving as liaison between school and community, taking on oversight of the learning garden's maintenance, and responding to teachers' needs as they work on integrating the learning garden into their curricula scope and sequence and around the district's assessment schedule.

Yet even as the need for implementing support staff is recognized, the practice is evolving. As more teachers make the garden part of their teaching practice, expanding garden-based education to an even wider variety of curricula and teaching styles, the role of the garden coordinator will undoubtedly continue to change.

TRAINING AND CURRICULUM

All five organizations profiled in this book assert that classroom teachers are key to sustaining children's access to the garden experience. Whether the program is grounded in health and food education or improving science outcomes, each of the case studies illustrates strategies to build teachers' capacity to use the learning garden with district curriculum. As Boston Schoolyard Initiative Education Director Kristin Metz says, "Teaching outdoors is more nuanced and complex a skill than usually assumed, especially in an urban public school. What we learned is that a teacher could believe it was important, could take the kids outside, could see the kids' excitement, but still not know what to do."

CitySprouts, the Boston Schoolyard Initiative, and REAL School Gardens have taken different approaches to address this challenge.

CitySprouts provides its partner schools with on-site support through a garden coordinator, supplemented when possible with more formal professional development for teachers at the district level. The goal is to establish garden-based learning by utilizing the resources schools already have as much as possible. Each garden coordinator is assigned to support a cluster of four schools (a total of one full school day a week at each school) with additional support from other CitySprouts staff and its FoodCorps service members. Throughout the year, garden coordinators meet with teachers individually or in grade-level planning meetings to highlight garden connections to specific units that align with the school's learning garden and with the season.

Meanwhile, another level of support for teachers is happening at the district level in collaboration with the science department. In 2010, when district science educators created garden extensions to the existing curriculum, the science department and CitySprouts co-led a series of school-based professional development sessions to introduce these "curriculum connections" to teachers. The support is extensive but effective: CitySprouts' partner schools consistently report on average 80 percent or higher teacher use of the learning garden.

The Boston Schoolyard Initiative, on the other hand, did not provide school-based support staff to schools. With an experienced curriculum developer on staff (Education Director Kristin Metz), BSI developed new science and literacy units designed for the schoolyard (with or without a BSI outdoor classroom). These were offered to all teachers through the district's professional development program for in-district credit. These schoolyard science and writing modules remain available to teachers through the Boston Public Schools science department and the BSI Web site, which will remain active until 2018. The science modules also have national exposure as a FOSS resource. In 2012, 69 percent of teachers reported using their schoolyard learning garden for science instruction.[3]

REAL School Gardens' approach to building teachers' capacity has the farthest reach of all, with support provided to more than one hundred public schools in Texas, and as of the 2014–2015 school year, a school in Washington, DC. REAL School Gardens devotes an intensive three years of support to its partner schools to get them up and running with garden-based education. REAL School Gardens and the school mutually select science units to extend to the new learning garden. The school then commits its entire staff to participate in a full-day training to introduce them to these science units. Two other training sessions follow, with smaller groups of teachers at the school that have self-selected for additional support and the option of one-on-one mentoring to teachers. Finally, after the three-year period schools can elect "Evergreen support," a lighter touch of ongoing support to keep teachers' garden use active. Like CitySprouts, REAL School Gardens reports a high percentage of teachers—more than 50 percent each year—utilizing their learning gardens for instruction. But it achieves this with intensive training sessions rather than the presence of a school-based garden coordinator.

PEER-TO-PEER LEARNING: A KEY INGREDIENT

Another way all three organizations build teachers' capacity for garden-based learning is by having teachers learn directly from one another. Formalizing this sharing of best practices, or creating a community of practice among teachers, is in itself a best practice reflected in several of the stories here. CitySprouts has explored several different options toward this end, including using a webinar series for teachers to share their own garden-based lessons and teaching strategies. Sam Ullery notes how much DC garden coordinators in the district appreciate having time together to share at OSSE garden coordinator monthly trainings. Kristin Metz remembers the momentum BSI gained from a group of Boston teachers who met regularly to solve problems and share best practices.

In the case of REAL School Gardens, the very program itself emerged from the community of practice made up of that first pioneering group of teachers working with Suzy Rall Peacock. From their informal gathering to learn more from one another to the nearby environmental conferences about outdoor education, these Texas teachers crafted a "practice" that ultimately became REAL School Gardens.

Whether in formal or informal contexts, teachers and garden coordinators sharing directly with one another seems to be a key ingredient for sustaining teachers' active use of the garden. All of these efforts, however, are vulnerable as districts make changes in learning standards and curricula is subsequently replaced or reduced. Science instruction is especially at risk, as schools have been forced to allocate more time to literacy or math. Sometimes, as history makes clear, science in the elementary grades all but disappears. Such circumstances mean that teachers have to start all over learning a new curriculum that may not allow for the same opportunities for experiential learning in general and garden-based learning in particular. As much as these school partnerships have accomplished, they are still at the mercy of a volatile educational policy climate.

THE FUNDING CHALLENGE

School garden programs have to support the same general areas: curriculum development (or adaptation to the garden), professional development to train and support teachers in using the garden, and not least, support staff to help teachers and oversee garden maintenance. In terms of revenue, it is significant that each program covered here is supported by a combination of public and private funds, reflecting the current state of garden-based learning—on the edge of gaining public commitment, but still reliant on the initiative of individuals. In short, garden-based education is a social investment on the cusp of public acceptance.

Education Outside and REAL School Gardens receive some funding from the school district budgets (or individual school budgets) in exchange for the service they provide to teachers and students in that district. CitySprouts has a service contract with the Cambridge Public Schools district toward the same end.

The Boston Schoolyard Initiative was funded through a public/private partnership between the City of Boston Mayor's Office and a philanthropist collaborative, with the majority of the funding going to the design and construction of outdoor classrooms in the city's public schools. Likewise, the schoolyard learning gardens in San Francisco used by Education Outside's partner schools were built with a portion of public funds made available through a series of city bond issues.

The OSSE School Garden Program, the only program among the five that is wholly within a public office (the Office of the State Superintendent of Education), is fully funded by public money secured through the DC Healthy Schools Act to improve children's healthy food access and education. The OSSE School Garden program, in fact, actually gives money back to school garden partners in Washington, DC, through a grant program to help support the garden coordinator position and make modest improvements to the learning gardens. It is an innovative, cost-effective means to support garden-based learning in public schools.

Compared to the cost of integrating technology into public schools, the cost of garden-based education is modest. Still, it is a significant challenge to today's public education funding systems, and if garden-based learning is going to expand and deepen, it needs the stability of a lot more institutional support at the district and state level.

ASSESSMENT

Funding is often the driver behind what outcomes a program measures. Bridget Rodriguez is director of planning and collaboration in the Massachusetts Executive Office of Education. She is also a former school principal, a former CitySprouts board member, and a Cambridge school parent. As a result, she has a uniquely multifaceted view of institutional garden-based education. "I think that supporting any additional cost in the bottom line of schools is going to be a challenge when you're working with limited resources," Bridget reflects. "But that's not specific to garden programs, or CitySprouts. It's generally an issue and I think that the more it can be tied to the outcomes for kids, it's easier to make the argument that that's a good investment."[4]

Indeed, all five programs have made documenting results a priority. Together, they look for outcomes across the three areas of garden-based learning: academic achievement, improved health and diet, and environmental knowledge and awareness. However, the emphasis varies in each program and, as Bridget implies, is related to where the bulk of the program's funding comes from. For instance, the programs that get funding from schools and district contracts primarily measure academic achievement and document how much or in what way teachers are using school gardens for instruction. OSSE, as might be expected, has a much stronger focus on how school gardens in the district are improving children's food choice and, ultimately, their health. The problem here is that no single program gets public funding for both academic and health outcomes even though both areas of change are core goals of our public school system. There is a danger that future garden-based learning programs will be more limited in scope unless public schools broaden what they ask for and what they are willing to pay for.

CONCLUSION

Ultimately, it's experience in the field that will guide our strategy as we integrate garden-based learning in public school education. Although they have some differences on the surface, the five organizations discussed in this book have much in common at the root level. They share a belief that teachers are gatekeepers to their students' learning experience. They know that a curriculum can support or hinder garden-based learning depending on how "receptive" it is to experiential learning strategies. They've established that training for teaching in the learning garden makes a difference: teachers who've participated in training really do use the garden more. They've demonstrated that it's important to broaden garden-based learning to teachers beyond the pioneers and early adopters; teachers need opportunities to learn from each other, and this type of learning is effective. Lastly, all five organizations are committed to exploring a combination of design and maintenance plans to keep learning gardens growing that don't rely on teachers to shoulder the bulk of the work.

These five programs also tell us something about the relationship between garden-based learning and public school culture. We can see that schoolyard learning gardens often serve as a bridge between school and neighborhood. We can also see that certain principles of learning garden design may be more important than actual infrastructure. Even very simple learning gardens can still be effective teaching resources and learning spaces for children.

Finally, these organizations reflect a range of approaches and strategies that illustrate that there is no single, right way. In fact, flexibility in how garden-based learning is implemented is absolutely essential if it's going to work for the many ways that individual school cultures differ, even among schools in the same district. Garden-based learning can thrive whether a school has high parent involvement or not, for schools with or without active afterschool programs, and in schools ready to support cafeteria staff active in promoting healthy food choices—but also in schools where the garden is more clearly aligned with academic outcomes. Successful school garden programs, in short, reflect many of the various subtle and not-so-subtle differences between school cultures.

CHAPTER 6

Policy and the Future of Garden-Based Learning

Imagine a teacher in an urban school who regularly uses his school garden for his fifth graders' science, math, and writing lessons. He is acutely aware that many of his students are struggling to master the academic skills they'll need to be successful in middle school and beyond. He is convinced that the hands-on approach of his garden-based lessons helps *all* of his students—struggling or not—to understand the concepts he's teaching. Further, this teacher feels that his fifth graders' connection to the edible vegetables and herbs in the garden and their expanding interest in the natural world has brought a cohesiveness to his class that makes them feel like they are working together as a real team. Being in the learning garden has awakened their interest in the world and sparked thoughtful conversations all around.

This teacher may feel isolated in his appreciation of the learning garden, but in fact larger policies have shaped his practice, like the kinds of educational resources he's expected to use in his teaching practice, how his students' families are invited to participate in the school community, and the quality of food his students are served in the cafeteria.

Sometimes the impact that policies have on school communities is limiting. They can add one more thing that a teacher is responsible for and held accountable to, regardless of whether those outcomes are within his or her control. But policies can also expand a teacher's practice. In the case of garden-based education, they can make it easier for a teacher to begin incorporating the learning garden into children's education, and they can help make garden-based learning possible to sustain. Education policy can, for instance, ensure that teachers are given adequate time and training to learn new strategies. Agricultural policy can encourage funding for locally grown food in the cafeteria and for the kind of kitchen equipment needed to prepare fresh produce. Environmental policy can broaden the scope of learning standards. Policy can even provide funding for school gardens or school garden partnerships.

Each of the areas that has shaped our modern learning gardens—academic achievement, food and health education, and environmental literacy—has in turn been shaped by policies that have made it easier or more difficult for a school community, district, or region to sustain active garden-based learning. Each view considers the learning garden a little differently, colored by its particular focus on food and health, nature and environmental literacy, or academic achievement. Looking at them all together gives us a fuller, more nuanced picture of how certain policies have encouraged or hampered school gardens in the past thirty years, and how they might impact the integration of garden-based learning in schools moving forward.

EDUCATION REFORM

Since *A Nation At Risk* was published in 1982, educational standards for children's academic achievement have shaped school culture and transformed teachers' practice in the classroom.[1] In 1994, an amendment to the Elementary and Secondary Education Act (ESEA) required states to set standards for what all children should know by the time they graduated high school.[2] The No Child Left Behind Act in 2001 (NCLB) echoed this theme of equitable education opportunities for all children by further requiring all states to set a definition for "proficient" academic achievement and then report their students' (including all subgroups) progress toward these goals each year.

It is impossible to consider a systematic integration of garden-based learning in teachers' practice without also considering how the nature of that practice has been shaped by these events in the standards movement. NCLB had a radical impact on school culture, whether viewed from the perspective of families, students, or teachers. Before NCLB, teachers often chose their own curriculum and made their own decisions regarding how they would translate it into instruction. After NCLB, in an attempt to ensure that all groups of children were succeeding, more districts moved to a districtwide curriculum and directed professional development for teachers around districtwide initiatives. Districts began making many of the decisions that used to be in teachers' purview, even as teachers were still held accountable for how their students performed on the tests that drove all of these changes. This, in turn, impacted the amount of control a teacher had over how the classroom was set up and how children's time was structured throughout the school day. When student assessment results failed to show improvement (or showed improvement, but too slowly), teachers were further directed to implement classroom changes mandated by the district or state. The standards-based movement narrowed opportunities for experiential learning as teachers experienced a profound loss of control over their choice of instructional strategies, classroom projects, and even lesson units. These changes in turn radically impacted how children and their families experienced school. A teacher who witnessed this shift describes a typical classroom in her school before NCLB: "When you came into a classroom, you could tell *like that* what we were studying because it was all around the room. You would *never* read a story about a pumpkin without having a pumpkin in the room." But that changed after the advent of NCLB. "Now we have a whole cohort of teachers who don't know about [project-based learning]. Teachers aren't comfortable going outside. It's a whole other wonderful space, but teachers aren't used to being asked to use it."[3]

These changes also transformed the relationship between public schools and the community groups that work closely in them. As children's time in and after school was scrutinized for how it supported academic achievement, programs for art education, music, and even social studies and science were reduced or eliminated to make more room for reading and math, the two subjects assessed for NCLB.[4] The time children were allotted for lunch shrank as schools searched for ways to maximize "learning time," forcing health advocates to collect evidence that eating a healthy lunch also had an impact on learning. As recess, too, came under attack, they gathered more evidence to prevent children's recess breaks from disappearing from the school day.[5]

Not all educators viewed garden-based learning as incompatible with learning standards. In 1994, Delaine Eastin, then California state superintendent of instruction, led an initiative to establish a school garden in every school in California. With over nine thousand public schools in the state, this represented by far the most extensive garden-based learning effort in the country. Although it was established first as a health and nutrition initiative (it was coordinated by the California Department of Education Nutritional Services), it also aspired to have an impact on children's academic needs. Eastin clearly saw school gardens as a vehicle for academic achievement. In an educational era rushing toward standards, Eastin framed California's school gardens as a tool not only for promoting health and nutrition but also for teachers to implement academic standards.

> Although I was a leading advocate of standards in order to ensure a higher quality education for all our children and to keep California's economy competitive, I increasingly recognize there is a danger that the standards will become a series of rote lessons. A garden in every school is even more essential to make our standards come alive. We must not lose the creativity, problem solving, and sheer love of learning that comes from hands-on, experiential learning.
>
> Gardens should not compete with our standards; gardens should be an avenue to high standards.[6]

Despite Eastin's optimism, integration with academic goals in the era of standards has proved difficult. Even as California passed a bill to fund school gardens, the challenges the bill aimed to address began with children's diet (in the face of an alarming increase in obesity rates) and secondly addressed their agricultural knowledge (as agricultural land increasingly was converted to development). Funding for the five thousand "instructional gardens" in California public schools was meant to support academic subjects as well as health, but even as the physical school gardens expanded, funding dedicated to professional development for teachers in using them failed to keep pace. A 2008 report showed that 80 percent of the funds requested by schools were for equipment or materials compared to only 19 percent for professional development.[7] Funds were largely used to build more school gardens and not, as Eastin had imagined in 1995, to integrate garden-based learning in teachers' practice.

In 2014, the standards movement evolved again with the rollout of the Common Core State Standards for math and language literacy and concurrently, the creation of the Next Generation Science Standards. Politically, Common Core differs from NCLB in that it was developed not by the federal government but collectively by state leadership. Common Core reflects more input from educators across these states, and adoption is by states' choice rather than federally mandated like NCLB. Common Core differs from NCLB in content, too: it spells out learning goals not just for knowledge but also for educational practices. It underscores the importance of applying knowledge and solving problems in real-world situations. It reduces the number of topics teachers are expected to cover so that students have a better chance of understanding "core" ideas. It expands the responsibility for students' competency in literacy from just English teachers to include science and social studies teachers, a concept that is echoed in the Next Generation Science Standards. Further, both the Common Core and Next Generation standards emphasize that all teachers share responsibility for English language learners mastering standards in literacy.

These are all changes that align with garden-based learning. Teachers already know the garden is a place filled with potential projects that combine skills and knowledge in a way that makes sense to children, from writing narratives in science journals that describe seasonal changes to learning about plant growth by growing a crop of salad greens for a spring "salad party."

The learning garden is also a constant source of real-world problems for students to solve—for example, addressing an invasive plant species in the garden such as Black Swallowort, or recognizing that cabbage moths indicate the probability of cabbage worms feeding on the tender plants, or creating an irrigation system to keep the garden watered.

Reducing the number of topics teachers are supposed to cover in a year is meant to allow a class to explore topics in depth, which can mean time to make a lesson-related trip to the schoolyard garden or incorporating a garden-based project into a unit.

Teachers have already discovered that the learning garden helps connect subject areas like science and literacy. It opens a world for children to discover through hands-on exploring, nonfiction reading, and descriptive writing. The emphasis Common Core and Next Generation place on English language learners' (ELL) literacy competency adds weight to teachers' perceptions that garden-based learning has particular value for their ELL students. Studies from the Boston Schoolyard Initiative, REAL School Gardens, and CitySprouts all confirm that teachers believe that hands-on lessons in the learning garden make a difference for students whose first language is not English, a demographic expected to increase in nearly every part of the country.[8]

Resistance to an expanded emphasis on experiential learning sometimes comes from traditionalists who fear it will compete with old-fashioned rote learning, or caution from educators who see it implemented in culturally restrictive ways that can further divide students.[9] And the fact remains that in the limited time in the school day, an experiential learning approach can compete with other initiatives that a district is compelled to support.

Still, there are signs that the Common Core and Next Generation standards foreshadow a curriculum trend to include more experiential learning strategies such as inquiry and project-based learning, sparked by recent research on how children learn. The FOSS outdoor science extensions, for instance, are now widely available to teachers around the country. As the FOSS Web site explains, "In recent years, it has become clear to us that we have a larger responsibility to the students we touch with our program. We have to extend classroom learning into the field to bring science concepts to life. In the process of validating classroom learning among the schoolyard trees and shrubs, down in the weeds on the asphalt, and in the sky overhead, students will develop a relationship with nature."[10] These FOSS outdoor lessons were piloted in Boston's outdoor classrooms (and created in collaboration with the Boston Schoolyard Initiative). Urban school districts that had eliminated experiential learning approaches twenty years ago may be inviting some of them back in. Boston Public Schools, for instance, has developed a new kindergarten curriculum that incorporates project-based learning and children's play, *Focus on K2*. One of the three units, Earth, encourages teachers to take students outside into the schoolyard to explore the natural world in their community.

Like other educational reforms before them, Common Core and Next Generation will be successful only if they gain the support of policy makers, school leaders, parents, and teachers. But they also allow for the possibility that a systematic integration of garden-based learning in public education could, in fact, become a significant element of how standards are implemented.

HEALTH AND WELLNESS POLICY

Nothing has shaped the current school garden movement more than edible education, which has redefined school gardens in the public eye since 1995 when Alice Waters joined forces with the Martin Luther King Middle School in Berkeley, California, to create the Edible Schoolyard school garden and program. Waters was already renowned as one of the founders of the modern local food movement. A restaurant chef-owner in Berkeley since 1971, Waters was known as a leading voice for organic growing practices in agriculture and sourcing ingredients locally. She influenced a change in the public's perception of food for health, gustatory, economic, and ultimately political choice. Waters's collaboration with Neil Smith, principal of the public middle school Waters passed on her way to work each day, became a flashpoint for teachers, parents, and health advocates who saw a bigger role for schools in children's food education. Alice Waters's leadership has impacted the economy of farmers, chefs, farmers' markets, and grocery stores nationally. She brought the force of the local food movement to school gardening and introduced a new audience of parents, health experts, and food activists to school gardens when she defined school gardens as critical places for children's food education. "What we are calling for is a revolution in public education—the Delicious Revolution. When the hearts and minds of our children are captured by a school lunch curriculum, enriched with experience in the garden, sustainability will become the lens through which they see the world," Waters said.[11]

Edible education has inspired numerous programs and individual efforts in edible schoolyards across the country and elevated "knowing where their food comes from" as a key cultural value for children as well as adults. As much as any event, it has defined school gardens as a response to the alarming rise in childhood obesity and diet-related illness over the past thirty years, and a more generalized concern over the American diet and how we eat.

In 2012, the Federal School Lunch Program nutrition standards were overhauled—for the first time in fifteen years—when the Obama administration ushered in new dietary guidelines, reducing salt and increasing whole grains and vegetables in many school lunch menus.

But getting healthier food is only part of the solution. More children will eat well—and start to make healthier choices as they get older—if healthier food choices are accompanied by food education. This has raised the question about the relationship between children's food experience at school and how families eat at home. Few would claim that the school garden is sufficient in itself to bring about a transformation in how families eat, but many school garden advocates are joined by health experts in their belief that school food and the culture of food at school is a potentially powerful agent for change.

The effort to address children's health has been given a boost with First Lady Michelle Obama's Let's Move campaign, started in 2009, to "raise a healthier generation of kids." Food and nutrition in school are one of the focus areas of the campaign, which also includes more physical activity for kids and less screen time. The First Lady's partnership with a nearby fifth-grade class to plant and harvest a vegetable garden on the lawn of the White House is a highly visible symbol for engaging children in growing food as a means to healthier diet choices. On a national level, the Farm-to-School Program reflects a federal recognition of the potential of public schools to improve children's health through food education. The USDA, home of the National Lunch Program, established the National Farm-to-School Program in 2000 to help get locally and regionally sourced foods into public school food service as well as to support schools' food education efforts to encourage children to make healthy food choices. The program received federal funding for the first time in 2004 through the Child Nutrition Reauthorization Act.

The collaborative Farm-to-School Network began in 2007 with the mission to promote farm-to-school projects around the country and to coordinate resources to help these grassroots efforts flourish. It covers local food procurement for schools' breakfast and lunch programs, school-based education programs for nutrition and food systems, and the creation of edible school gardens that can serve in a number of ways (including augmenting children's meals at school and educating students about how food is grown in their community). School gardens have been an important venue for Farm-to-School. In a 2013 census of over 13,000 school districts nationwide, 43 percent (38,629 schools) reported that they were engaged in some kind of farm-to-school activity, and 13 percent (3,473 schools) reported that they had school gardens in their school district.[12]

In 2011, FoodCorps established itself as a national AmeriCorps initiative to improve children's education about and access to healthy, locally grown food in high-need communities around the country. FoodCorps focuses on three areas of action: providing food and nutrition education for children, building and tending school gardens in high-need schools, and increasing the shift toward healthier food in school cafeterias. FoodCorps places its 125 service members in a year of service at one of 108 partner sites, spread across 15 states. These sites include afterschool programs, farm-to-school programs, and nonprofits working in schools—a network of efforts focused on the role of food in children's health. Both CitySprouts and the OSSE School Garden Program incorporate FoodCorps service members in their programs.

Twenty years later, it's clear that Delaine Eastin was right. School gardens can work as an instructional resource for teachers and at the same time work for edible education. What is also clear, however, is that edible education would be strengthened if it could be more systematically tied to teachers' practice. The tight academic focus of the standards-based curriculum-and-assessment cycle has so dominated teachers' practice and students' time that it is hard for teachers to adapt their core academic lessons to garden programs primarily focused on local food procurement and healthy eating. The challenge is to integrate edible education with standards-based school culture so that it becomes a regular feature in children's elementary education. Health and wellness outcomes are as critical to children's healthy development as academic outcomes. Garden-based learning can deliver on both.

ENVIRONMENTAL EDUCATION POLICY

Environmental education is a subject area that touches both the natural and social sciences; it concerns the impact of nature on people and vice versa. Today's school-based environmental education is often about expanding children's conception of the natural environment beyond the schoolyard to include places that are uncultivated, or "wild." For urban children who haven't traveled beyond their city's limits, seeing natural habitats near and far from where they live can be life-changing. Trips to museums open their eyes to the depth of study around a specific environmental topic like animals or climate. A visit to nearby wetlands or urban wilds can fundamentally shift their understanding of the world we live in. Such field trips are a different kind of learning experience than stepping out into the schoolyard with the class. In a garden bed, there is an ongoing series of tasks and projects to do—turning the compost, adding it to the soil, planting and cultivating, harvesting, and then starting all over again. In a natural habitat, children have to take a very different approach in order to maintain the ecosystem they find. That means observing rather than digging, identifying what's growing rather than selecting what to plant, and recognizing the signs of decomposition. Environmental education in our schools ideally encompasses both kinds of habitats and both kinds of interaction with nature.

With the advent of the twenty-first century, connecting children to nature has taken on a more urgent tone. Richard Louv's 2008 book, *Last Child in the Woods*, galvanized people with its characterization of children's access to nature as squeezed between the technology that increasingly keeps kids indoors and the steady encroachment of development on wild and uncultivated places. Louv makes clear the impact this shift is having on the healthy development of our children. An environmentally illiterate society also raises serious concerns for our future in general.

School gardens are recognized as an effective way to illustrate to children one critical aspect of our relationship to nature. They show a natural habitat that humans have cultivated for their sustenance and pleasure. School gardens help children understand the connection between food systems and personal health (in other words, where our food comes from and the choices we make about eating) and how food systems are connected to the health of our planet. Garden-based learning is an indispensable tool for environmental education.

The school garden increasingly has the potential to connect to environmental practices inside the school as well. A good example of this is the Green Schools initiative, a movement propelled by the design and construction of environmentally compatible school buildings, from how they are built to their ongoing energy use (such as maximizing solar energy to reduce energy loss). In addition to holding environmental events for students and advocating for environmental education, sometimes Green Schools also incorporate educational programming to extend the facility's "greening" to the school's educational purpose, with a particular emphasis on science, technology, engineering, and math (STEM). It's an approach to environmental education that starts from the practicality of building facilities and moves toward pedagogy. While there is no dedicated public funding for the Green Schools initiative, there are at least twenty-one state networks throughout the country sharing best practices and coordinating resources.[13]

There is another nationwide effort in environmental education, however, that specifically focuses on education policy. The No Child Left Inside Act (NCLI) is a proposed amendment to the Elementary and Secondary Education Act to provide support for environmental education programs in public education. Supported by the NCLI Coalition, a national group formed in 2007 to advocate for environmental education, the effort comprises state-specific groups working to get support for NCLI from their state's elected officials. Key provisions in the NCLI legislation are support for each state in developing an Environmental Literacy Plan that details how it will integrate environmental literacy concepts into core academic programs in public schools; funding for teacher training; and capacity grants to scale up best practices in environmental education. As much as garden-based learning is a tool for integration, NCLI would clearly help support this strategy for teachers. The funding promised in NCLI would also appear to bolster the efforts of schools to use the schoolyard (including the garden) to support environmental practices inside the school and in the larger community.

NCLI clearly weighs in on a question that environmental education has grappled with for over a decade: whether environmental learning standards should exist as distinct standards or be integrated with existing education standards. This was a question that the Pew Charitable Trusts sought to answer in a 1995 study on the impact of environmental education on core academic learning. A landmark for environmental education, *Closing the Achievement Gap: Using the Environment as an Integrating Context for Learning* remains a seminal study of the effects of environmental education on students' core academic learning. The Pew study concluded that environmental learning standards should be integrated into existing academic subjects rather than stand alone. Not all educators agreed, however. Two states took the other tack and established environmental standards as a distinct standard: in 2002, the State of Pennsylvania incorporated environment and ecology standards as a fourth strand in its educational goals (after math, reading, and science). In 2003, the State of California established the Education in Environment Initiative (EEI) to supplement its existing educational standards.[14] However, the trend continues to lean toward integrating environmental learning standards in traditional academic subjects. A current running through the Next Generation Science Standards, for instance, is understanding the "impact of the environment on humans, and the impact of humans on the environment." Understanding our relationship to the earth and our dependence on its resources is increasingly seen as a key concept in science education.

The escalating changes in the earth and its climate call for a different kind of knowledge. Just as importantly, they call for a different way of *thinking*. As anyone even cursorily following the news can see, the decisions that ordinary citizens make will have a profound effect on life as we know it, from the pace of climate change to how we secure healthy food sources all over the world. Understanding science, and environmental issues in particular, is an important twenty-first-century skill for us to master. Our public education needs to reflect this from the time children begin school. Garden-based learning is one way we can prepare for that.

CONCLUSION

Health and wellness, environmental education, and education reform are three lenses through which to view the goal of healthy development for our children. Together, they create a vision for our future. In this world, our children understand and hold reasoned opinions about environmental issues, both locally and globally. They have a knowledge base from which they can make thoughtful decisions about how best to protect the earth's natural resources, including our food systems. In this vision, all of our children grow up with practice making healthy decisions about what they eat. They are conscious of *how* they eat, too—the social elements of eating, like knowing how to prepare a meal and making time to sit down with others to eat. They are able to hold their own against the onslaught of a billion-dollar advertising industry attempting to influence their food purchases. In this imagined world, there is a system for universally and equitably ensuring that all of our children have access to the knowledge and experiences they need to make good choices for lifelong health, find meaningful work and relationships, and steward natural resources. That system would be our public schools.

We have too often viewed academic achievement, health education, and environmental awareness as distinct areas of children's development, with well-intentioned advocates competing for one or another as the priority area. In truth, life experience usually blurs these boundaries. Children's intellectual growth, good health, and their understanding of human reliance on nature may in fact all be improved when they are allowed to stew in the mix of real-world "learning experiences." What an impact our schools would have if edible education advocates built on the tenets shaping education reform; if school reform advocates fought as hard for science education as they do for math and literacy achievement; and if environmental advocates recognized food systems as a core element of what children need to know about the natural environment. Garden-based learning is a teaching strategy that helps to make these connections. When it is in teachers' practice as part of standards-based lessons, the learning garden is accessible to a lot of children—in effect, every child who's exposed to standards-based curriculum. When it is situated in an edible garden, food and growing are woven into the tapestry of how children learn, and all of this takes place in the context of the interrelated systems of our natural world.

Garden-based learning is a tool whose value is not fully recognized in any of the three areas. But it should be. It's effective in engaging children's curiosity. It gives children a reason to learn and opportunities to practice the skills they need. It gives them a base of knowledge from which to draw. It connects these three areas in ways that further the goals of each. More collaboration and a broader focus would go far toward creating a strong future for all our children.

CHAPTER 7

Ripe for Change

THREE THINGS EDUCATORS CAN DO
AND THREE LESSONS THEY CAN APPLY

Going outside to the schoolyard garden with a class is like taking a field trip without leaving school. It feels like an entirely different learning space than the classroom and yet it is only moments away. Class in the learning garden is not recess; it's lesson time, and often on the same subjects that students are reading about in books back in the classroom. But now they are outside—with garden beds instead of desks, in the fresh air, surrounded by animals seen and unseen.

Nature is where we all, at the most basic level, live. It's important to know that, and also to *feel* that. Years ago, I spent an afternoon with a group of eighth-grade boys digging up potatoes. They were amazed to find potatoes growing underground and surprised by their almost peppery flavor when we cooked and ate them. I've witnessed a third grader who struggled with the answer (in English, that is) to lessons in class but could speak with authority about the decomposition process in the compost bin in the garden. I recently met a seventh-grade girl with an impressive knowledge of flowers she'd never seen. She liked drawing flowers in art class, so she'd learned about them entirely from an Internet search. Not every child is drawn to the garden so passionately, but all children are greatly enriched by directly experiencing it. They deserve opportunities like this to realize that they, too, have a fundamental relationship to the natural world. As the Next Generation Science Standards so aptly put it: the natural environment has an impact on us, and we have an impact on it.[1]

I began this work from my perspective as a parent inspired by my children's teachers. Teachers are often the first adults our children form relationships with outside of their family. They help our young children make their first friends, guide them toward healthy choices about what to eat, and encourage healthy, physical play. They inspire our children to become readers and writers, and give them skills to navigate the literate world for the rest of their lives. They witness the normal yet profound changes our children go through in just one grade year of development; we depend on them to respond to many, many more facets of our children's development beyond academic knowledge. Imagine the challenges teachers face in addressing so many different kinds of children, from so many backgrounds, coming to school with such varied learning styles and emotional states. Collectively, we're counting on teachers to be our partners in helping every child in their class to grow up smart, strong, and kind.

Garden-based learning is a tool teachers need for today's students, and it's an experience all children deserve. Clearly, the learning garden is adaptable to different student populations and sensitive to the hugely divergent levels of "readiness" with which children begin school. It levels the playing field and equalizes opportunities for all children. It is clearly time to build on the work of our modern pioneers in garden-based learning to make it a teaching practice that's supported throughout our public education system.

Garden-based learning is an example of a practice that truly blossoms in the hands of a skillful teacher. But this book has shown that teaching in a garden can become something every teacher does. It's a practice with historical roots in education that has new relevance today. It's a strategy that can broaden the "entry point" for children's interest in a subject, making it clear to young people how the knowledge and skills they're being taught in the classroom can be useful for their world outside the classroom, too. The learning garden gives young people a real-world application to many skills educators have identified as key: inquiry, observation, and knowledge about the natural world (such as changes over time, how plants reproduce and grow, ecosystems, and how social systems connect). The school garden can become a vital resource to teachers held accountable for these common skills and knowledge standards. Garden-based education combined with skillful teaching can be powerful change agents.

It is abundantly clear that garden-based education teaches important lessons about health and wellness, too—for example, how to make healthy food choices, the implications of what we eat, and our diet's impact on our lifelong health. Just as importantly, the garden puts food in the context of our environment as children learn firsthand how food grows, what it tastes like when it's harvested, and that the garden is a system in that its parts work together to create something wholly different than what they are separately. For urban children with few other opportunities to simply explore a safe, outdoor space, this can be profound on both a personal and a societal level, as our world increasingly needs an environmentally literate citizenry.

We're at an inflection point that involves expanding the role of garden-based learning beyond the small band of early-adopter teachers already convinced of its value. Children, like gardens, grow and change constantly; they will not wait for another thirty years as we continue to put together a system based on the isolated brilliance of our current practice. Getting education right for all of our children is urgent. The opportunity to create a broad-scale implementation of garden-based education in the classroom will slip away unless we act now. This chapter will outline three steps we can take to help get all of our children access to garden-based academic learning, edible education, and environmental literacy. It will also reflect on the precedent of integrating (now near-ubiquitous) technology in the classroom, lessons we can apply moving forward, and the resources that will be required to meet our goal of access for all children.

1. SPEAK UP

The standards movement that began in 1982 grew in response to disturbing evidence that many of our children were graduating from our public school system without the knowledge and skills they needed for career, college, and civic engagement. The subsequent reform effort was made exponentially harder because there was no national agreement on what children should know or be able to do after thirteen years in our public school system (and there still isn't). Our public education system in 1982 was designed as if most children would grow up to live and work in the same community where they went to grade school when, in fact, that was not (and is not) the reality. It was a system that appeared to hold different standards for students depending on their race and socioeconomic background. For the students who came in with less, our public schools generally offered less. In a nation built on the principles of fairness, this education reform movement demanded that communities respond to the academic needs of every group of children in their community. The premise in the standards movement to address these wrongs is something every thinking person can get behind.

But just as important as holding to this premise until things are made right is insisting that education reform is shaped by what we know now—thirty-five years later—and the ways that schools have changed. We know that student academic assessments should have enough "data points" to capture learning from the variety of curricula teachers use, including experiential-based curricula. What's more, schools should be evaluated on school climate as well as student achievement. We have an obligation to make all of our schools healthy places for children to be. This means feeding children school lunches that meet *at least* basic nutritional standards. We should insist on adequate schoolyard recess spaces and time to play outside. We must also insist on schoolyard learning gardens and time to learn outside. But it's not enough for our schools just to be healthy places. We have a second obligation to make all of our schools places where children learn about good health. Physical education and food education at school will support the next generation's habits of lifelong health.

There is a role for educators in this effort. Garden-using teachers need to be talking about what they do and sharing what they've learned, recognizing that garden-based learning is more than a personal choice—it's a viable strategy for public education. Teachers were the first advocates for learning gardens and they will always be at the center of the movement. We need principals to nurture school environments that support garden-based learning, protect time for teachers to learn and practice, and encourage a community of practice for teachers to share. There is growing evidence showing the particular and urgent value garden-based

learning has in children's education, but there is not yet a strong educator voice insisting that every teacher has access to a schoolyard learning
garden and every district has curricula encouraging teachers to extend
lessons outside.

The standards outlined in Common Core refer to the extensive research showing the value of experiential learning strategies in children's learning; the school garden is cited as a good example of the kind
of informal learning environment teachers are encouraged to build into
their students' experience. It is a particularly accessible informal learning environment that is adaptable to classroom projects or extensions
to more traditional curriculum. Either way, children are gaining meaningful access to the outdoors. That is something all educators should
fight for.

There is also a role for those served by schools—that is, families. As
this book has made abundantly clear, teachers' time with our children is
shaped by national, state, and district directives. That, in turn, affects
children's access to the garden during the school day. Families need to
advocate for teachers' voices in school reform, supporting good practices
that teachers have developed. Parents should recognize how important
garden-based learning is for all children—not just our own—and act ac-
cordingly.

Integrating garden-based learning on a big scale will help make the
practice stronger in every child's classroom. Broad-scale integration of
the learning garden means that teachers have the time to take a lesson
outside, and to prepare and train for organizing and managing a class
in the garden. Students' learning in the garden needs to be reflected in
the assessments upon which the teacher's job is based. Without a system that values experiential learning strategies, garden-based learning
has no long-term home in teachers' practice. And without a strong connection to teachers' practice, school gardens will remain outside most
children's experience. It's a very positive sign that health and wellness
is increasingly recognized as having a place in public education. Institutional support for garden-based learning in teachers' practice will create
a foundation for sustainable food and environmental education in public schools.

2. INVEST

Like school libraries and computer labs, learning gardens are a fundamental resource for teachers and need to be developed and maintained
as such. We need to invest in public schools to create and maintain
schoolyard learning gardens as a core part of school facilities. What ex-
actly each school or district needs may vary depending upon the climate,
environment, and school culture. As the examples in this book show,
learning gardens can—and should—reflect all the ways that schools
and communities differ from each other. But underlying the wonderful diversity in the learning gardens themselves must be a commitment
to creating and then maintaining them. Designing, building, and maintaining a schoolyard learning garden can overwhelm a school or community partner but is not such a big hurdle when it is considered part of the
overall district facilities responsibilities.

The cost of public school learning gardens falls into two primary cate-
gories: designing and building the learning garden, and providing training and ongoing professional development for teachers. Maintenance
falls between these two. Both primary costs need to be built into city
and school budget plans. Boston and San Francisco are setting a precedent for public investment in schoolyard learning gardens that are designed for teachers' curricula. These gardens have natural habitats and
edible growing spaces that serve as a palette for teachers' instruction.
Pathways are wide and stable against the elements. They include seating within the garden suited to the writer-workshop style of instruction that these districts use. The infrastructure of a schoolyard garden
is fairly straightforward: paths, beds, plants, water. It becomes "active"
as these static elements interact with nature (this part is free of charge).
Compared to a school library or computer lab, after all, the costs for installation are relatively low.

As with the computer lab, the cost of training and supporting teachers in using the learning garden is significantly higher than installing
the resource but absolutely essential to getting the value from it. Studies
from the Boston Schoolyard Initiative and REAL School Gardens confirm that training is key to garden use. In fact, BSI's study showed that
teacher training was a more reliable indicator of teachers teaching out-

side than the existence of a schoolyard learning garden. Support staff for teachers is part of the program cost. Garden maintenance in two of these models (CitySprouts and Education Outside) is partly absorbed in the support staff. In the models described in this book, garden educators on a per-school comparison cost significantly less than information technologists and librarians. As with any investment in schools, costs are ultimately weighed against academic outcomes in students. In this light, garden-based learning is a remarkably efficient use of public money. Like the school library or computer lab, it should become an educational resource that all public school teachers can count on.

As the examples in this book show, public funding for garden-based learning can take many forms and connect to a range of outcomes: an investment in the public school facility, as well as improvements in health and nutrition and students' academic achievement. Collectively, these examples set a precedent for viable ways communities can build a base of public support for garden-based learning in their schools. Without the public commitment to garden-based learning and the school garden, garden-based education will be perpetually out of reach of teachers for whom it could be a unique and valuable tool. More importantly, it will remain out of reach for the vast majority of public school students, many of whom would benefit from it in extraordinary ways.

We've seen a tremendous interest in school gardens over the last decade, as indicated by the private funding that got a lot of school garden programs started and continues to sustain the majority of programs featured in this book. But if this private investment doesn't transition to significant public funding, the trend will come and go even as the need for garden-based learning continues to increase. "You need to know that the resource is going to be there day in and day out," Cambridge Public Schools' Lisa Scolaro notes. "Because you invest this time, you don't want to see a year from now 'Oh, there's no garden.' And feeling confident that you work in a place that will support that is a necessary piece. Funding disappears left and right . . . you have to feel that it's not going to go away, because it takes a lot of work to make meaningful connections." Public funding for garden-based education is essential.

3. LEARN MORE

When schools make decisions about how scarce resources are allotted, outcomes matter. Garden-based learning is a promising initiative that uniquely addresses a host of different facets of children's development. But as an emerging practice, it does not yet have the weight to stand up competitively to other initiatives. Teachers' testimonials are tantalizing, as are families' perceptions that the school garden is vital. These are compelling reasons for a serious inquiry about the role of garden-based learning in the outcomes we're witnessing.

There are many thousands of school garden programs happening all over the country (3,473 counted in the 2013 Farm-to-School school garden census). We need to know more about how these school garden programs work, what they have in common, and how they differ from one another. We need to know what outcomes they consider important. We should know how these garden programs are currently integrating with their school's core curricula, how teachers find the school garden effective (and in what areas), and if others find a similar correlation between outcomes and garden-based instruction. We need a tool that accounts for the many variables in school cultures around the country, and even within the same state or district, because these variations will be important in helping us understand what makes garden-based learning so valuable to children.

In a 2013 synthesis of garden-based education from 1990 to 2010, Dr. Dilafruz Williams, Professor of Educational Leadership and Policy at Portland State University, and her coauthor P. Scott Dixon confirmed that teachers and garden-based educators are confident that the school garden has an impact on children's learning, their relationship to nature, and their food choices. At the same time, Williams and Dixon decried how little this body of research has captured. "Although the growth of school gardens, garden programs and activities, garden curriculum, and garden-based learning is laudable, the movement falls short in that there has not been a parallel focus on rigorous research to understand the academic learning outcomes in a systematic manner," they write.[2] The authors note that ethnicity was mentioned in only a third of the studies, and socioeconomic status was considered as a variable in only a "cursory manner" in the research. Their conclusion, which I share, is that there is an open field for future study in garden-based education.

Research not only lays the foundation for future teachers' practice but also shapes how we can most effectively support today's garden-using teachers. For instance, it's clear that a sustainable garden practice in public education needs additional support staff to help teachers, but what should that position look like for optimum impact? Can support staff take on other responsibilities, like food education, that are currently not being addressed by school staff? As we realize the importance of health education in school, are there other staff roles that need to be filled? If so, how can garden support staff integrate with them? In short, research provides an important container to hold the range of experience now taking place as well as directing our efforts for the future. It's important that practices and outcomes accumulating from the good work of garden educators around the country now are examined for clues to widespread, sustainable implementation.

The work of thirty-plus years of our modern school-garden pioneers is too valuable not to take further. Answers to these questions will surely highlight some existing best practices and, equally important, will tell us new things about how the garden supports children's learning. If the school garden movement is to take root, to really be accessible to communities currently unfamiliar with the phenomenon, then we need to learn more and have strong evidence for an investment in garden-based education.

A PRECEDENT: LESSONS FROM THE COMPUTER LAB

It might seem impossible to change the view of garden-based learning from something that's good but not essential to something that we just can't live without. It may seem like a pipe dream that all schools have learning gardens along with the infrastructure to keep them growing and integrated with the knowledge and skills children need to develop in the twenty-first century. But there's a precedent for just such a phenomenon: the introduction of computers into elementary school classrooms. Technology's integration into public schools is an initiative that took root in public school culture and grew to become a central tenant of twenty-first-century learning.

The first personal computers were introduced to the public in the 1980s, about the same time that *A Nation At Risk* shook public education.[3] Throughout the decade, technology became part of children's lives at home (the first video games became commercially available in 1972)[4] and at school (in the early 1980s, Apple computers were marketed to public schools through special low-cost programs). Technology appears explicitly in the learning standards for elementary students in the 1993 Benchmarks for Science Literacy, and in the 1996 National Science Education Standards, signifying a blending of science and technology—and there were earlier efforts to integrate technology with social studies standards, too.[5] In the mid-1990s, technology was transformed by the World Wide Web, which enabled people to access a flood of information as well as to connect and communicate with others in unprecedented ways.

Beginning in 2001, school reform also underwent a dramatic shift as No Child Left Behind was rolled out across the country. Schools increasingly had access to the Internet and began to build it into their administrative systems (sharing information), use it for their communication systems (such as email), and integrate it with instruction as education software continued to develop. Starting in 1994, the U.S. Department of Education began to monitor whether public schools provided computer and Internet access to their teachers and, increasingly, if they provided it to their students. By 2000, 97 percent of public elementary school teachers reported they had access to computers or the Internet somewhere in their schools, a dramatic rise from only 30 percent in 1994.[6]

The story sounds like an unstoppable wave of integration, but Betsy Corcoran, in *A Brief History of (Edtech) Time*, describes it more as a series of tides as she outlines some of the obstacles schools faced in integrating technology in the classroom.[7] Technology was an emerging industry in the 1980s directed toward businesses, which had more leeway than schools to experiment with brand-new tools to their trade. Teachers had (and still have) little time in their schedule for exploring new media, especially first-generation computers and software that had yet to be shaped by the experience of real students' needs. What's more, Corcoran points out, stakes start off high for teachers willing to pioneer new instructional practices with untried technology and emerging software. They have just a school year in which to make sure their students master grade-level skills; and when children don't do so in that small window of time, it can set them back for years. "Such conditions meant that the teachers who pioneered innovative uses of computers in their classrooms in the late 1980s and early 1990s were truly exceptions," Corcoran writes. "They poured extraordinary effort into their work, and frequently burned out. Although many became local heroes, few could create systemic change. When they inevitably left their schools their programs withered."

Funding for technology and education reform was anything but steady in these decades, a factor that impacted both the development of education technology and its subsequent integration in schools. In the 1990s, investment in tech startups coincided with investments in education innovation like Teach for America and the Knowledge Is Power Program (KIPP), which attracted a wider audience to elementary education and public schools. The crash in tech stock value in 2001 led to investors' retrenchment; the recession in 2007 likewise severely impacted funding for public school budgets. But less than a decade later, the tide turned again for technology integration when funding for twenty-first-century skills, including skills in technology, flowed through the federal Race to the Top initiative and private sources like the Bill and Melinda Gates Foundation. And as public schools were increasingly expected to produce measurable results in exchange, Corcoran notes, "reformers looked to technology to bolster teachers."

By 2010 the general public began to experience a wave of breakthroughs in technology: smartphones harnessing computer service to access and share information, and new and improved search engines to channel and organize information. More affordable technology lowered the threshold for startup businesses, which in turn fostered more software development. With close to 97 percent of teachers reporting they had access to the Internet and computers, education technology being piloted in classrooms, and 40 percent of teachers reporting that they often used classroom computers during instructional time, it's clear that many of the initial hurdles of forty years ago have been overcome.

Technology is described in the Common Core as a tool to access reading, writing, speaking, and listening. The Partnership for Assessment of Readiness for College and Careers (PARCC) proposes to replace annual paper-and-pencil assessments with online tests for students around the country, making computer skills a necessary condition for measuring students' literacy and math skills.

As it became more and more necessary for schools to integrate technology in their curriculum, equitable access to this new resource became an issue. Federal funds (through the E-rate program) were made available to schools with populations of 50 percent or more low-income students, and additional funds if schools were in rural areas. A second measure of access is how many classrooms ("instructional rooms") had access to the Internet—a critical component if teachers were to incorporate it into lessons they led in their classrooms. Results in 2000 show significant disparity between schools based on the income level of their students and in schools where more than half the students were minority. Recent studies have shown that it's not just access to technology that is influenced by socioeconomic status but also how children with different resources are taught and encouraged to use it.[8] There is as much power differential in the use of technology, it turns out, as there is in access to the equipment. This finding echoes studies on how food education influences healthy eating purchases beyond just the availability of healthy food.

Lesson #1: The Value of Resiliency and Engagement

Both technology and ecology encompass knowledge and skills close to the pulse of our fast-changing world. They are particularly relevant to the twenty-first century. In nature, we observe fundamental processes to life, like food growing from the earth and the cycle of growth and decay and then growth again. Until now, we could assume that people were growing up with a familiarity with nature, and so were able to build from that base of experience. We cannot live without natural resources, but this fact does not seem to be entirely understood by today's young population. As a society, we are losing resiliency—the ability to respond and adapt to changing circumstances in ways that keep life-supporting systems intact. An environmentally literate and *engaged* citizenry is an absolute essential in a future that is increasingly confronted with extreme weather, floods and drought in unexpected places, and ever-scarcer natural resources.

Lesson #2: The Importance of Equal Access to Both Tools and Knowledge

The integration of technology in schools shows us that our children need more than access to a resource, they also need education about engaging with it—in this case, education about natural systems, including food systems. For at least thirty-five years, we've recognized gaps in achievement between children who have cultural resources and those who have less. The most recent standards still acknowledge gaps in opportunity between demographic groups. Our public schools are the place we can address those differences, and our teachers are the ones who can do it if we give them the tools. In ecology as well as technology, those tools include curriculum that allows for experiential learning, training in how best to implement it, and time and a place—the schoolyard learning garden—to practice it. The question of equitable access to knowledge, and gaining experience in employing it, is one that schools are in a unique position to address. The broad steps in the integration of both technology and ecology are strikingly similar: creating the resource (computer labs and learning gardens); integrating the new field of knowledge and skills with existing standards and expectations (notably, both have a natural home in science, as well as connections to other subjects); carving out the time in the school day for use; and training teachers and developing the position of support staff (information technologists and garden coordinators).

The introduction of computers into public schools illustrates that change, even in an institution as decentralized as elementary education, can happen quickly if the need for it is clear, it is built into learning standards, and it is established as a tool that teachers and students require for learning. The assumption that all schools should make *technology* accessible to both teachers and students is now the norm. We are facing a unique opportunity to do the same for *ecology*.

Lesson #3: The Necessity of Combining Public and Private Funding

It takes a combination of private and public funding to establish a new initiative broadly and equitably. The ability to integrate technology into schools over a thirty-year period was partly the result of a combination of private and public funding supporting different parts of the effort. It was not a steady stream of money, as the story illustrates. "Steady" is not a necessary condition; a more important factor is having a combination of public (in this case, federal) funding complemented by private sources (largely foundations) that can fill in and respond to each other and thereby move the initiative toward its goal.[9] Computers in schools, for instance, would never have spread without the help of federal funding to ensure that low-resourced schools got Internet access through the E-rate program. But making computers affordable through a combination of philanthropy and the marketplace was an essential complement to those federal funds. Both of these pieces should be in place for garden-based education, too. As Betsy Corcoran succinctly points out, teachers need scaffolding to make technology (and ecology) systematic. Pioneers are not an example of "anyone can do it" but rather part of a heroic effort to make a system available to all.

CONCLUSION

Fifteen years ago, I dove deep into garden-based learning, though I wouldn't have called it that at the time. Like many other volunteers in school gardens in early 2000, I was thrilled to be a part of taking children outside to a place as beautiful as a garden during the school day. I had no real sense of the complexity of public school culture, of what challenges teachers faced in building a classroom culture, in helping twenty-five or more children from very diverse backgrounds relax into learning, and engaging students in their various points of interest to get them to meet roughly the same learning goals by the end of the year. I only knew that the dozen teachers I met were as excited as I was by the children going to the garden. When we came back to the classroom, I watched these teachers connect that garden experience to reading, writing, numeracy, and science. I saw the deftness with which a teacher could transfer a child's excitement being in the garden into developing writing skills, vocabulary, counting and sorting skills, and an understanding of the carbon cycle. To the children, learning these skills made sense because they had a problem to solve or a place they wanted to know more about. To the teachers, they now had students eager to tackle a challenge that would have otherwise been overwhelming. As for me, I was hooked.

The more I've learned about garden-based learning, the craft of teaching, and public school culture over the past fifteen years, the more certain I am that this is a tool from which every teacher can benefit. The changes we've all witnessed in that same time convince me that every child desperately needs the experience of learning outside. I believe that integrating garden-based learning in our public school system is entirely possible to achieve if enough of us see the value in it. We are at a point of transition in two places: elementary education and our relationship to our increasingly fragile environment. Now is the time to address *both* points by advocating for the changes that can make garden-based learning an everyday occurrence for all of our children. It is entirely within our grasp.

APPENDIX A

Sample Teacher Usage Surveys

These are two examples of surveys given to teachers, from CitySprouts and REAL School Gardens, that collect information about how teachers use their school garden for instruction. The surveys reflect the similarities and differences in how each program offers support for garden-based learning.

EXHIBIT A.1
CITYSPROUTS TEACHER SURVEY 2014

Name: _____ School: _____

Grade and/or subject: _____

Thank you for taking the time to complete CitySprouts' annual survey to teachers in our partner schools. Our CitySprouts staff supports teachers in connecting their standards-based lessons to the school garden in four ways:

- Collaborating with teachers to plan and implement a garden-based project, lesson, or activity in the school garden
- Assisting as teachers lead a class outside in the garden
- Making an "expert visit" to the classroom, or bringing garden materials inside
- Ensuring that the school garden meets the needs of teachers

Your response to the questions below are very important to us in measuring how well we're achieving our program goals and also help us improve our support to you in using your school garden for teaching.

1. Did you use your school garden for a teaching activity this year?
   ___Yes ___No

2a. If yes, approximately how many separate visits did your class make to the school garden this year?   ___(# visits)
   These times include teaching in the garden with or without the garden coordinator, classroom activities that utilized material from the garden, or a classroom visit from the CitySprouts garden coordinator or FoodCorps.

2b. Of these visits, how many were made **without** the garden coordinator?
   ___(# visits)

3. What subjects did you teach in the garden? **Check all that apply:**
   ___SCIENCE (e.g., insect/butterfly life cycle; plant life cycle; soil; weather)
   ___MATH (e.g., counting, sorting, estimating; measuring; graphing)
   ___ENGLISH LANGUAGE ARTS (e.g., descriptive writing; process writing; journaling)
   ___SOCIAL STUDIES (e.g., colonial history; Three Sisters; cultural connections to home countries)

4. Are you using your school garden **more** than you did last year?
   ___ Yes ___No

5. To what extent do you agree with each of these statements?
   Please circle one. (1=Strongly disagree, 2= Disagree, 3= Mixed/ Neutral, 4= Agree, 5= Strongly Agree)

5a. The garden is an effective tool for students whose first language is **not** English.
   Circle one: 1 - 2 - 3 - 4 - 5

5b. The CitySprouts program helps me meet my students' learning goals.
   Circle one: 1 - 2 - 3 - 4 - 5

5c. Garden-based instruction contributes to my students' interest in the content of the lesson.
   Circle one: 1 - 2 - 3 - 4 - 5

5d. I feel my students are more likely to retain knowledge learned through garden-based lessons than in lessons that do not have hands-on activities.

　　Circle one: 1 - 2 - 3 - 4 - 5

5e. I feel that the school garden experience increases my students' curiosity in the natural environment.

　　Circle one: 1 - 2 - 3 - 4 - 5

5f. I feel that the time we've spent in the school garden this year has increased my students' comfort in being outside.

　　Circle one: 1 - 2 - 3 - 4 - 5

6. What other ways has the garden changed your students' experience?

Questions or comments:

Please return this survey by Wednesday, June 4th, to your garden coordinator or to the CitySprouts mailbox in your school's main office.

Thank you!

Source: CitySprouts

EXHIBIT A.2
REAL SCHOOL GARDENS
PROFESSIONAL DEVELOPMENT SURVEY

Session title_____ Presenter name(s)_____

Your school _____

We'd like to learn something about your teaching practices during the time that you're involved with REAL School Gardens. A version of this survey will accompany each PD event you do with RSG. It's important that we be able to connect what you tell us now with what you tell us at prior and later dates. Because we don't ask for your name or other identifying information, we're asking you to please fill in the three pieces of information below. This will provide a unique but <u>anonymous</u> identifying code for you. This information will only be used to link your past, current, and later responses. It will not enable anyone to identify you by name. THANK YOU for helping to improve the program! NOTE: write an "x" if you don't know or if the answer is "none."

Your mother's *middle* name_____	The day of the month that your birthday falls on (1–31)____	Your father's *middle* initial ____

What is your role for the current school year?
    a. Teacher
    b. Administrator
    c. Other school staff
    d. Family member or other volunteer
    e. I'm not sure/these choices don't apply to me

How much do you disagree or agree? For each of the following items, please circle the one number that best matches your opinion.	Strongly DISAGREE	Tend to Disagree	Tend to Agree	Strongly AGREE	Not sure or N/A
PD1. This PD connected directly and explicitly with the state curriculum standards I am accountable to.	1	2	3	4	0
PD2. I will be able to apply the content of this PD to my regular work right away.	1	2	3	4	0
PD3. The presenter(s) did an effective job at leading the main session(s) I attended today.	1	2	3	4	0

PD4.   **In a couple of sentences, please describe the main idea, feeling, knowledge, or insight you are taking away from this session.**

PD5.   **Interest in future professional development offerings by REAL School Gardens**
   a. I am not interested in receiving further professional development regarding teaching outdoors/in my schoolyard.
   b. I would consider attending more REAL School Gardens professional development if my school and/or district offer it.
   c. I will definitely attend if my school and/or district offer more professional development with REAL School Gardens.
   d. I would like to take this opportunity to strongly encourage my school and/or district to offer more professional development with REAL School Gardens.
   e. I plan to actively explore developing an ongoing relationship with REAL School Gardens in order to take the learning from this session to the next level.
   f. I'm not sure, these choices don't apply to me, or I am taking this survey as a pre-evaluation for an upcoming professional development opportunity.

These next questions focus on your individual stage of action with respect to teaching outdoors/in gardens/in your schoolyard. All responses should refer to the current school year. For each item, please circle the one answer that best describes your opinion.

LM1.   **Subject area content knowledge**
   a. There is little to no connection between my curriculum/subject area(s) and teaching outdoors/in gardens/in our schoolyard.
   b. I have little to no training in content appropriate for teaching outdoors/in gardens/in our schoolyard, but I might be interested.
   c. I already have some ideas and plans to teach my primary content area(s) outdoors/in gardens/in our schoolyard.
   d. I regularly teach outdoors/in gardens/in our schoolyard and sometimes even integrate content across subject areas.
   e. I am becoming an expert at using the outdoors/garden/schoolyard to integrate content across subject areas.
   f. I'm not sure/these choices don't apply to me.

LM2.   **Beliefs about outdoors/gardens/schoolyards as resources for increasing student achievement**
   a. School gardens have very little to do with student academic achievement.
   b. I am interested in learning more about the academic benefits of teaching outdoors/in gardens/in our schoolyard.
   c. I believe there are academic benefits for students engaged outdoors/in gardens/in our schoolyard.
   d. I am increasingly excited about the positive academic outcomes for students as a result of our work outdoors/in gardens/in our schoolyard.
   e. Teaching children outdoors/in gardens/in our schoolyard is one of the best ways I know for helping students learn.
   f. I'm not sure/these choices don't apply to me.

LM3.   **Engagement**
   a. I prefer to teach in an indoor environment.
   b. I have seen others who are very excited about teaching outdoors/in gardens/in schoolyards, and I am curious to learn more.
   c. I am convinced that teaching outdoors/in gardens/in our schoolyard will bring a new energy to my teaching, and I am planning on getting started soon.
   d. Teaching outdoors/in gardens/in our schoolyard energizes me and makes teaching more fun.
   e. My career as a teacher is much better because of my experiences with students outdoors/in gardens/in our schoolyard.
   f. I'm not sure/these choices don't apply to me.

LM4. **Teaching skills and methods**
   a. I feel unprepared to teach outdoors/in gardens/in our schoolyard.
   b. I am curious as to how teaching outdoors/in gardens/in our schoolyard might be similar to or different than teaching in a traditional indoor environment.
   c. With a little more development of my skills and methods I could begin teaching outdoors/in gardens/in our schoolyard soon.
   d. My teaching skills and methods have proven effective outdoors/in gardens/in our schoolyard.
   e. Student-driven inquiry provides the context for my lessons outdoors/in gardens/in our schoolyard.
   f. I'm not sure/these choices don't apply to me.

LM5. **Teaching tools and resources**
   a. I am not interested in curricula or other tools for teaching outdoors/in gardens/in our schoolyard.
   b. I am curious about what curricular/district support exists for teaching outdoors/in gardens/in our schoolyard.
   c. With a few good lesson plans I could begin teaching outdoors/in gardens/in our schoolyard soon.
   d. I plan successful experiences for my students outdoors/in gardens/in our schoolyard with current resources, but I am always seeking additional curricula and tools.
   e. I have a well-developed "toolkit" for teaching outdoors/in gardens/in our schoolyard.
   f. I'm not sure/these choices don't apply to me.

LM6. **Time spent teaching outdoors**
   a. I don't teach outdoors/in gardens/in our schoolyard.
   b. Teaching outdoors/in gardens/in our schoolyard is interesting, but I don't really have the time.
   c. I teach outdoors/in gardens/in our schoolyard fewer than six times per year.
   d. I teach outdoors/in gardens/in our schoolyard more than six times per year.
   e. I teach outdoors/in gardens/in our schoolyard so often that it is like having a second classroom.
   f. I'm not sure/these choices don't apply to me.

D3.   **In terms of my overall curriculum plan for the current school year, teaching and learning outdoors/in gardens/in our schoolyard is:**
   a. A very small part of it, if at all.
   b. A significant but contained unit.
   c. A major part of it.
   d. The core organizing structure.
   e. I'm not sure/these choices don't apply to me.

Anything else you'd like to share? We really value your comments, feedback, questions, and quotable summary statements. We are especially interested in critical comments about what did NOT work well or what could be improved.

THANKS AGAIN for taking the time and effort to complete this survey!! Your responses will help improve REAL School Gardens. Please return completed surveys to a REAL School Gardens staff person.

For office use only:	**Session type**
	a. Teacher to teacher (T2T)
Date_____	b. New school partner on-site PD
	c. 3rd or 5th year cohort PD
Admin notes:	d. School-sponsored training event
- THANKS (teacher time and effort is a gift to the program)	e. District-sponsored training event
- Confidential (no one connects responses to individual people)	f. Community-wide training event
- Use (continually improve PD offerings, track long-term impact)	g. Digging for TEKS
	h. Other (specify) _____

Source: PEER Associates/REAL School Gardens teacher survey

APPENDIX B

Cambridge Public Schools Curriculum Connections

The Cambridge Public Schools Science Department educators created a series of lesson extensions for science units at each grade level, kindergarten through eighth grade. Each of these "curriculum connections" highlights points in the unit where a school garden activity has the potential to enhance students' understanding of a particular concept or skill.

EXHIBIT B.1
GRADE 3 PLANT GROWTH AND DEVELOPMENT— GARDEN CONNECTIONS

Lesson	Lesson description	GC role
1	*Lesson 1:* Students communicate their ideas about plants and what they know and want to find out. *Garden connection:* Class visits the garden and goes on an introductory tour with garden coordinator or teacher.	GC leads tour if necessary.
2	*Lesson 2:* Students record observations of seeds, compare seeds, draw and label parts of seeds. *Garden connection:* Class visits garden to observe seeds (either on plants or in saved seed collection).	GC coordinates seed locations (either living or saved) with teacher.
3	*Lesson 3:* Students record observation of the life cycle of a plant; observe development of leaves, buds, and flowers. *Garden connection:* Class visits the garden to observe and sketch plant life cycle stages.	GC and teacher communicate about where to find plants in different stages of growth.
4	*Lesson 4:* Students share information about bees and observe bees/insects pollinating plants. *Garden connection:* Class visits garden to observe pollinators. (NOTE: Pollinators may or may not be active, depending on season, weather, time of day, etc.).	GC and teacher communicate about best locations/times to observe pollinators.

Lesson	Lesson description	GC role
5	*Lesson 5:* Students could observe and sketch other insects found in the garden and observe and record data about insect behavior in garden. *Garden connection:* Class visits garden to observe insects.	Not necessary.
6	*Lesson 6:* Students observe details of the anatomy of a flower; draw and label parts of the flowers. *Garden connection:* Class visits garden to observe live flowers or pick three or four flowers per class to observe (to minimize number of flowers being picked). (NOTE: Flowers may or may not be blooming, depending on timing of lesson.)	GC and teacher communicate about best flowers to observe.
7	*Lesson 7:* Students could sketch another flower and label parts and compare and contrast the anatomy of the flowers. *Garden connection:* Class visits garden to observe live flowers or pick three or four flowers per class to observe (to minimize number of flowers being picked). (NOTE: Flowers may or may not be blooming, depending on timing of lesson.)	GC and teacher communicate about best flowers to observe.
8	*Lesson 8:* Students observe development of fertilized pods; record, draw, and graph growth and observations. *Garden connection:* Class visits garden to observe fertilized seed pods (either on plants or in saved pod collection).	GC coordinates pod locations (either living or saved) with teacher.
9	*Lesson 9:* Students harvest seeds, count and compare seeds, and record observations. *Garden connection:* Class visits garden to harvest seeds. (NOTE: Seeds may or may not be available on live plants, depending on timing of lesson.)	GC and teacher communicate about seeds to harvest (if available on live plants, or in saved collection).
10	*Lesson 10:* Students could observe, measure, and sketch plants in the garden weekly to make connections to plants that are growing in the classroom. *Garden connection:* Class visits garden weekly to observe, measure, and sketch plants in the garden.	Not necessary.
Weekly	*Lesson (weekly):* Teachers can emphasize that all our fruits and vegetables start with seeds and that some of our food is grown in gardens like this!	

Source: © Cambridge Public Schools Science Department (Cambridge, Massachusetts).

APPENDIX C

OSSE School Garden Assessment Template

The OSSE School Garden Program has created this assessment tool to guide and evaluate the many school partners providing support and coordination to its city's schools.

EXHIBIT C.1
DC SCHOOL GARDEN ASSESSMENT

(See table on following pages)

Indicator	Exceeds	Working toward	Does not meet	Missing	Comments
DESIGN					
Circulation	Walkways allow students to experience the garden through the use of all senses and are well defined. The width, materials used, and placement of walkways reflects the intended use. (8 points)	Walkways allow students to experience the garden through the use of some senses OR are not well defined, OR the width, materials used, and placement of walkways somewhat reflects the intended use. (3)	Walkways allow students to experience the garden through the use of few senses AND/OR are not well defined AND/OR the width, materials used, and placement of walkways does not reflects the intended use. (1)	This component is missing. (0)	
Seating	Seating is age-appropriate and is available for the expected number of students who will use the garden at one time. Seating is shaded and multipurpose, and promotes reflection, observation, and conversation. (5)	Seating is somewhat age-appropriate OR is not available for the expected number of students who will use the garden at one time. OR seating is not multipurpose OR seating is not shaded OR does not promote reflection, observation, and conversation. (3)	Seating is not age-appropriate AND is one of the following: is not available for the expected number of students who will use the garden at one time; is not multipurpose; is not shaded; does not promote reflection, observation, and conversation. (1)	This component is missing. (0)	
Signage	Signage is age-appropriate and student-centered. An entrance sign is a permanent, multiuse structure that is clearly visible and actively promotes vision, open hours, current happenings, maintenance tasks, contact information, and upcoming events. Educational signs are in place throughout the garden and enhance the educational experience of the space. (5)	Signage is somewhat age-appropriate and student-centered. An entrance sign is either not a permanent OR multiuse structure OR it is not clearly visible OR it does not actively promote vision, open hours, current happenings, maintenance tasks, contact information, and/or upcoming events. OR there are few educational signs throughout the garden. (3)	Signage is not age-appropriate and/or student-centered. An entrance sign is either not a permanent OR multiuse structure OR it is not clearly visible OR it does not actively promote vision, open hours, current happenings, maintenance tasks, contact information, and/or upcoming events. AND there are few educational signs throughout the garden. (1)	This component is missing. (0)	
Meeting Area	The central meeting area is a multiuse space that supports the maximum number of students who will use the garden at one time. There is a white/chalkboard clearly visible. Class supplies such as notebooks, writing utensils, and teaching materials are easily accessible. Systems are in place for students to efficiently transition in and out of this space. (8)	The central meeting area is a somewhat multiuse space OR it does not support the maximum number of students who will use the garden at one time. OR there is no white/chalkboard clearly visible. OR class supplies such as notebooks, writing utensils, and teaching materials are not easily accessible. OR systems are somewhat in place for students to efficiently transition in and out of this space. (6)	The central meeting area is not a multiuse space OR it does not support the maximum number of students who will use the garden at one time. Two of the following are true: there is no white/chalkboard clearly visible OR class supplies such as notebooks, writing utensils, and teaching materials are not present OR systems are not in place for students to efficiently transition in and out of this space. (3)	This component is missing. (0)	

Component				
Tool Storage	Tool storage is in a weatherproof structure, is easily accessible, is well organized, and contains appropriate tools. Tools are organized for maximum efficiency and systems are in place to ensure for proper tool care and use. (8)	Tool storage is in a somewhat weatherproof structure, OR is not easily accessible, OR is not well organized, OR does not contain appropriate tools. AND/OR tools are not organized for maximum efficiency OR systems are somewhat place to ensure for proper tool care and use. (6)	Tool storage is not in a weatherproof structure, OR is not easily accessible, OR is not well organized, OR does not contain appropriate tools. AND tools are not organized for maximum efficiency OR systems are not in place to ensure for proper tool care and use. (3)	This component is missing. (0)
Security Features	Garden is highly visible from nearby public spaces. Tools are secured safely. No hazards area present. (10)	Garden is somewhat highly visible from nearby public spaces. OR tools are not secured safely. No hazards are present. (7)	Garden is not highly visible from nearby public spaces. AND tools are not secured safely. OR hazards are present. (3)	This component is missing. (0)
Accessibility	All components of the garden are readily accessible to the target audience, including those with disabilities. Regular open hours are maintained. (9)	Some garden elements are inaccessible to the target audience OR those with disabilities do not have garden access. OR regular open hours are not maintained. (7)	Many garden elements are inaccessible to the target audience AND/OR those with disabilities do not have garden access. AND/OR regular open hours are not established. (4)	This component is missing. (0)
SYSTEMS				
Soil	Soil tests and observations show the soil has sufficient macro and micro nutrients and proper structure and pH to meet plant needs. A detailed plan is in place to ensure that soil health is maintained. (10)	Soil tests and observations show the soil has insufficient macro and micro nutrients and proper structure and/or pH to meet plant needs. OR an underdeveloped plan is in place to ensure that soil health is maintained. (7)	Soil tests and observations show the soil has severely insufficient macro and micro nutrients and proper structure and/or pH to meet plant needs. OR no plan is in place to ensure that soil health is maintained. (3)	This component is missing. (0)
Biologic	Plants are diverse and appropriate for the intended use of the garden resulting in high yields and vigorous growth. Planting areas are weeded/cared for regularly. Plants are properly sowed, maintained, and harvested. (10)	Plants are somewhat diverse and appropriate for the intended use of the garden resulting in moderate yields and growth. OR planting areas are weeded/cared for irregularly. OR Some plants are not properly sowed, maintained, and/or harvested. (7)	Plants are not diverse and inappropriate for the intended use of the garden resulting in poor yields and growth. OR planting areas are not weeded/cared for. OR many plants are improperly sowed, maintained, and/or harvested. (3)	This component is missing. (0)

Indicator	Exceeds	Working toward	Does not meet	Missing	Comments
Pest & Disease Management	Plants are healthy and no serious pest or disease problem exists. An organic management plan is in place that effectively manages pests and diseases. (10)	Plants are somewhat healthy and no serious pest or disease problem exists. OR an organic management plan is in place that somewhat effectively manages pests and diseases. (7)	Plants are unhealthy and serious pest or disease problem exists. OR an organic management plan is not in place. (3)	This component is missing. (0)	
Wildlife	Wildlife is regularly spotted in the garden. It is a sanctuary for wildlife with pollinator plants, plants that attract beneficial insects, and homes for native birds. (10)	Wildlife is not regularly spotted in the garden; however, attempts have been made to create a sanctuary for wildlife with pollinator plants, plants that attract beneficial insects, and homes for native birds. (7)	Wildlife is not regularly spotted in the garden, AND no attempts have been made to create a sanctuary for wildlife. (3)	This component is missing. (0)	
Water	The garden employs an effective watering system that is appropriate for the scale, type, and purpose of the garden. Students are trained in proper watering techniques and are responsible for the watering. A plan is in place for watering over school breaks. (10)	The garden employs a somewhat effective watering system that is appropriate for the scale, type, and purpose of the garden. OR students are somewhat trained in proper watering techniques and are responsible for the watering. OR an ineffective plan is in place for watering over school breaks. (7)	The garden employs an ineffective watering system that is inappropriate for the scale, type, and purpose of the garden. OR students are not trained in proper watering techniques. OR no plan is in place for watering over school breaks. (3)	This component is missing. (0)	
Compost	The garden has a well-designed, maintained, effective compost system that produces high-quality finished compost. The system minimizes rodent issues. The compost system is appropriate for the size and type of garden. Students are trained on proper composting methods and are responsible for composting. (10)	The garden has a somewhat well-designed, maintained, effective compost system that produces finished compost. The system attempts to minimize rodent issues. OR the compost system is somewhat appropriate for the size and type of garden. OR students are not fully trained on proper composting methods and are not responsible for composting. (7)	The garden has a poorly designed, maintained, ineffective compost system that produces little finished compost. OR the system has rodent issues. OR the compost system is inappropriate for the size and type of garden. OR students are not trained on proper composting methods and are not responsible for composting. (3)	This component is missing. (0)	
Community Participation	The program is highly effective in involving community members through regular well-planned events. Communications are effective at reaching the community and are frequent and regular. (15)	The program is somewhat effective in involving community members through regular well-planned events. OR communications are somewhat effective at reaching the community. (10)	The program is not effective in involving community members. Events are not regular and/or well planned. AND communications do not reach the community. (5)	This component is missing. (0)	

PROGRAM ORGANIZATION

Vision Statement	A vision and mission aligns with that of the school. (5)	A vision and mission somewhat aligns with that of the school. (3)	A vision and mission that does not align with that of the school. (1)	This component is missing. (0)
Funding	A reliable funding source has been identified and the school's budget includes a line item for the school garden. The school regularly matches funds to support the garden program. (15)	A somewhat reliable funding source has been identified OR the school's budget does not include a line item for the school garden. OR the school does not match funds to support the garden program. (10)	Funding sources have not been identified AND the school's budget does not include a line item for the school garden. AND the school does not match funds to support the garden program. (5)	This component is missing. (0)
Institutional Support	The garden is well supported from the top down. The garden is a part of the school's vision/mission. (15)	The garden is somewhat well supported from the top down. OR the garden is loosely a part of the school's vision/mission. (10)	The garden is not supported from the school staff. OR the garden is not a part of the school's vision/mission. (5)	This component is missing. (0)
Garden Coordinator	A highly skilled dedicated garden coordinator is responsible for the day-to-day operations of the school garden and record keeping. This person is compensated for this time, receives training, and is supported by the school staff. (15)	A skilled garden coordinator is responsible for the day-to-day operations of the school garden and record keeping. This person is sometimes compensated, OR does not receive training, OR is unsupported by the school staff. (10)	A garden coordinator is responsible for the day-to-day operations of the school garden and record keeping AND this person is unskilled OR is not compensated, OR does not receive training, OR is unsupported by the school staff. (5)	This component is missing. (0)
Garden Committee	A garden committee is established with a vibrant school wellness committee and includes diverse representation that establishes and upholds the garden purpose, vision, and goals. (10)	A garden committee is established and includes somewhat diverse representation that establishes and upholds the garden purpose, vision, and goals. (7)	A garden committee is established but does not meet OR does not include diverse representation. (3)	This component is missing. (0)
Student Involvement	All students are involved in various aspects of the garden. (10)	Greater than 50% of the student body is involved in various aspects of the garden. (7)	Less than 50% of the student body is involved in various aspects of the garden. (3)	This component is missing. (0)
Maintenance Plan	A yearlong maintenance plan is in place that clearly defines responsibilities, work assigned, and tasks. Regularly scheduled work days are productive and well attended by the community. (15)	A yearlong maintenance plan is in place that clearly defines responsibilities, work assigned, and tasks. OR work days are productive and well attended by the community. (10)	A yearlong maintenance plan is not in place that clearly defines responsibilities, work assigned, and tasks. OR work days are irregular and/or not well attended by the community. (5)	This component is missing. (0)

Indicator	Exceeds	Working toward	Does not meet	Missing	Comments
INSTRUCTION					
Curriculum and Instruction	A standards-based garden curriculum is used to teach most garden lessons. Teachers use a wide range of instructional techniques in the garden. (25)	A standards-based garden curriculum is used to teach most garden lessons. Teachers do not use a wide range of instructional techniques in the garden. (17)	A standards-based garden curriculum is used to teach few garden lessons. AND teachers do not use a wide range of instructional techniques in the garden. (10)	This component is missing. (0)	
Teacher Involvement	Many teachers use the garden across subject areas. Professional development is available to all teachers, in which all teachers participate. The garden is used throughout the year. (25)	Some teachers use the garden across subject areas. Professional development is available to some teachers OR the garden is not used through the entire year. (17)	Few teachers use the garden or teachers from only one subject area use the garden OR limited professional development is available OR the garden is used for a very short period of the throughout the year. (10)	This component is missing. (0)	
Student Impact	The program has an overwhelmingly positive impact on student's attitudes and or behavior in a measurable way. (25)	The program has a somewhat positive impact on student's attitudes and/or behavior in a measurable way OR the program has an overwhelming positive impact on student's attitudes and behavior but this impact is not measurable. (17)	The program has a negative impact on student's attitudes. (10)	This component is missing. (0)	
IMPROVEMENT PLAN					
Improvement Areas (Pick 3)	☐ Circulation ☐ Biologic ☐ Institutional Support ☐ Seating ☐ Pest & Disease Management ☐ Garden Coordinator	☐ Garden Committee ☐ Meeting Area ☐ Water ☐ Student Involvement ☐ Tool Storage	☐ Compost ☐ Curriculum and Instruction ☐ Accessibility ☐ Community Participation ☐ Teacher Involvement	☐ Vision Statement ☐ Student Impact ☐ Maintenance Plan ☐ Security Features ☐ Signage	
Goals					
Technical Support Needed					

Source: District of Columbia Office of the State Superintendent of Education

Resources

Blair, Dorothy. "The Child in the Garden: An Evaluative Review of the Benefits of School Gardening." *Journal of Environmental Education* 40 (2009): 15–38.

Boston Schoolyard Initiative. http://www.schoolyards.org.

Bucklin-Sporer, Arden, and Rachel Kathleen Pringle. *How to Grow a School Garden: A Complete Guide for Parents and Teachers*. Portland, OR: Timber Press Inc., 2010.

CitySprouts. http://www.citysprouts.org.

Corcoran, Betsy. "A Brief History of (Edtech) Time." *Texas Education Review* 1 (2013).

Danks, Sharon Gamson. *Asphalt to Ecosystems: Design Ideas for Schoolyard Transformation*. Oakland, CA: New Village Press, 2010.

Eastin, Delaine. Introduction to "A Child's Garden of Standards: Linking School Gardens to California Education Standards," v–vi. Sacramento: Nutrition Services Division, California Department of Education, 2002.

The Edible Schoolyard Project. http://www.edibleschoolyard.org.

Education Outside. http://www.educationoutside.org.

FoodCorps. http://foodcorps.org.

Full Option Science System and Regents of the University of California. "Taking FOSS Outdoors." http://archive.fossweb.com/news/taking_foss_outdoors.html.

Green Schools National Network. https://greenschoolsnationalnetwork.org.

Jaffee, Roberta, and G. Appel. *The Growing Classroom: Garden-Based Science*. South Burlington, VT: National Gardening Association, 1990, revised 2007.

Life Lab Science Program. http://www.lifelab.org.

Louv, Richard. *Last Child in the Woods: Saving Our Children from Nature-Deficit Disorder*. Chapel Hill, NC: Algonquin Books, 2008.

National Farm to School Network. http://farmtoschool.org.

Office of the State Superintendent of Education. http://osse.dc.gov/service/school-garden-program-sgp.

REAL School Gardens. http://www.realschoolgardens.org/.

Slow Food USA. "National School Garden Program." http://gardens.slowfoodusa.org.

Sobel, David. *Place-Based Education*. Great Barrington, MA: Orion Society, 2004.

United States Department of Agriculture Food and Nutrition Service. "Farm to School." http://www.fns.usda.gov/farmtoschool/farm-school.

Williams, Dilafruz R., and P. Scott Dixon. "Impact of Garden-Based Learning on Academic Outcomes in Schools: Synthesis of Research Between 1990 and 2010." *Review of Educational Research* 83, no. 2 (2013): 211–235.

Notes

Foreword

1. Kevin C. Armitage, *The Nature Study Movement: The Forgotten Popularizer of America's Conservation Ethic* (Lawrence: University Press of Kansas, 2009).
2. H. D. Hemenway, *How to Make School Gardens* (New York: Doubleday, Page and Co, 1903).
3. Bill Bigelow, "How My Schooling Taught Me Contempt for the Earth," *Rethinking Schools* 1, no. 11 (1996).
4. Gregory Smith and David Sobel, "Bring It on Home," *Educational Leadership* 68, no. 1 (2010).
5. David Sobel, "You Learn What You Eat, Cognition Meets Nutrition in Berkeley Schools," *Orion Afield* v, no. 3 (2001).

Introduction

1. Janet Forté, interview by the author, January 24, 2014.
2. Henry Vandermark, in conversation with the author, July 19, 2010.
3. Sondra M. Parmer et al., "School Gardens: An Experiential Learning Approach for a Nutrition Education Program to Increase Fruit and Vegetable Knowledge, Preference, and Consumption Among Second-Grade Students," *Journal of Nutrition Education and Behavior* 41, no. 3 (2009): 212–217.
4. Kenneth Ginsburg, "The Importance of Play in Promoting Healthy Child Development and Maintaining Strong Parent-Child Bonds," *Pediatrics* 119, no. 1 (2007): 182–191.
5. Sam Dillon, "Schools Cut Back Subjects to Push Reading and Math," *New York Times*, March 26, 2006, http://www.nytimes.com/2006/03/26/education/26child.html?pagewanted=all.
6. John B. Diamond and James P. Spillane, "High-Stakes Accountability in Urban Elementary Schools: Challenging or Reproducing Inequality?" *Teachers College Record* 106, no. 6 (2004): 1156.
7. Michael Pollen, "The Food Movement, Rising," *New York Review of Books*, May 20, 2010, http://www.nybooks.com/articles/archives/2010/jun/10/food-movement-rising/.
8. Office of the Surgeon General (US); Office of Disease Prevention and Health Promotion (US); Centers for Disease Control and Prevention (US); National Institutes of Health (US), *The Surgeon General's Call to Action to Prevent and Decrease Overweight and Obesity* (Rockville, MD: U.S. Office of the Surgeon General, 2001).
9. United States Department of Agriculture Food and Nutrition Service, Farm to School Census (2014), question 14, www.fns.usda.gov/farmtoschool/census.

10. Whitney Cohen, telephone interview by the author, March 18, 2014.
11. Full Option Science System, "Taking FOSS Outdoors" (2012), https://www.fossweb.com/taking-foss-outdoors; National Research Council, *A Framework for K–12 Science Education: Practices, Crosscutting Concepts, and Core Ideas* (Washington, DC: National Academies Press, 2012), 70.

Chapter 1
1. National Center for Education Statistics, "Public School Enrollment," May 2014, grades preK–8, http://nces.ed.gov/programs/coe/indicator_cga.asp.
2. Dilafruz R. Williams and P. Scott Dixon, "Impact of Garden-Based Learning on Academic Outcomes in Schools: Synthesis of Research Between 1990 and 2010," *Review of Educational Research* 83, no. 2 (2013): 219.
3. David A. Kolb, *Experiential Learning: Experience as the Source of Learning and Development* (Englewood Cliffs, NJ: Prentice Hall, 1983), 20–25.
4. "Pioneers in Our Field: Friedrich Froebel—Founder of the First Kindergarten," *Early Childhood Today*, August 2000, http://www.scholastic.com/teachers/article/pioneers-our-field-friedrich-froebel-founder-first-kindergarten.
5. "Increasing Access to Full-Day K: A Key Strategy for Boosting Learning and Closing Achievement Gaps for Children," Children's Defense Fund, April 2012, http://www.childrensdefense.org/child-research-data-publications/data/increasing-access-full-day-k.pdf.
6. Melinda Wenner, "The Serious Need for Play," *Scientific American Mind*, January 28, 2009, http://www.scientificamerican.com/article/the-serious-need-for-play/.
7. Dorothy Blair, "The Child in the Garden: An Evaluative Review of the Benefits of School Gardening," *Journal of Environmental Education* 40, no. 2 (2009).
8. Ibid., tables 5 and 6, 28–30.
9. Williams and Dixon, "Impact of Garden-Based Learning."
10. Ibid., table 1, 220–221.
11. Blair, "Child in the Garden," 35.
12. Melanie LaForce and Liz Bancroft, *Science in the Schoolyard Evaluation: Final Report* (Chicago: Outlier Research and Evaluation, CMSE, University of Chicago, 2013), 12–19, http://outlier.uchicago.edu/BSI-SSY/about-evaluation/.
13. National Research Council, *Taking Science to School: Learning and Teaching Science in Grades K–8* (Washington, DC: National Academies Press, 2007), 24.
14. National Research Council, *A Framework for K–12 Science Education: Practices, Crosscutting Concepts, and Core Ideas* (Washington, DC: National Academies Press, 2012), 28.
15. Neil Schiavo, "Program Evaluation of CitySprouts and the Cambridge Public School District Science in the Garden Workshops" (January 2011): 4, http://www.citysprouts.org/wp-content/uploads/2011/05/CitySprouts_CPSD.evaluation.Final-report1.pdf; LaForce and Bancroft, *Science in the Schoolyard Evaluation*, 17.
16. Blair, "Child in the Garden," 33.

17. National Research Council, *A Framework for K–12 Science Education*, 280.
18. Blair, "Child in the Garden," 34.
19. Partnership for 21st Century Skills, "Framework for 21st Century Learning," March 2011, http://www.p21.org/about-us/p21-framework.

Chapter 2

1. National Research Council, *Taking Science to School: Learning and Teaching Science in Grades K–8* (Washington, DC: National Academies Press, 2007).
2. Susan Agger, interview by the author, December 18, 2013.
3. National Research Council, *Taking Science to School*, 19.
4. Neal Klinman, interview by the author, February 6, 2014.
5. Wisconsin Fast Plants, "History of the Wisconsin Fast Plants Program," University of Wisconsin-Madison, http://www.fastplants.org/about/about_the_program.php.
6. Kelly Petitt, interview by the author, February 4, 2014.
7. Dorothy Blair, "The Child in the Garden: An Evaluative Review of the Benefits of School Gardening," *Journal of Environmental Education* 40, no. 2 (2009): 16.
8. Donna Peruzzi, interview by the author, July 29, 2014.
9. Madhvi Patil, interview by the author, July 31, 2014.
10. Caitlin O'Donnell, interview by the author, January 27, 2014.
11. These are among the Common Core State Standards Initiative College & Career Readiness Standards for Speaking and Listening.
12. Massachusetts D.E.S.E. School/District Profiles, http://profiles.doe.mass.edu.
13. Dan Monahan, interview by the author, December 20, 2013.

Chapter 3

1. Dorothy Blair, "The Child in the Garden: An Evaluative Review of the Benefits of School Gardening," *Journal of Environmental Education* 40, no. 2 (2009): 16; Melanie LaForce and Liz Bancroft, *Science in the Schoolyard Evaluation: Final Report* (Chicago: Outlier Research and Evaluation, CMSE, University of Chicago, 2013), 28, http://outlier.uchicago.edu/BSI-SSY/about-evaluation/.
2. Neal Klinman, interview by the author, February 6, 2014.
3. National Research Council, *A Framework for K–12 Science Education: Practices, Crosscutting Concepts, and Core Ideas* (Washington, DC: National Academies Press, 2012), 26.
4. Blair, "The Child in the Garden," 32; LaForce and Bancroft, "Science in the Schoolyard Evaluation," 29.
5. Daniel Desmond, James Grieshop, and Aarti Subramaniam, *Revisiting Garden-Based Learning in Basic Education* (Rome: Food and Agriculture Organization of the United Nations, and Paris: International Institute for Educational Planning, 2004), 24.

Chapter 4

1. Ross Miller, email communication with author, April 24, 2014.
2. Kristin Metz, interview by the author, February 12, 2014.

3. Eric Vanderbeck ("Mr. V."), "Wet and Wild Water Education in Texas," REAL School Gardens blog, April 3, 2012, http://www.realschoolgardens.org/realstories/12-04-03/Wet_and_Wild_Water_Education_in_Texas.aspx.
4. Jeanne McCarty, interview by the author, May 19, 2014.
5. Joe Petner, interview by the author, May 1, 2014.
6. Neil Schiavo, "Program Evaluation of CitySprouts and the Cambridge Public School District Science in the Garden Workshops" (January 2011): 2, http://www.citysprouts.org/wp-content/uploads/2011/05/CitySprouts_CPSD.evaluation.Final-report1.pdf.
7. Lisa Scolaro, interview by the author, May 14, 2014.
8. Schiavo, "Program Evaluation," 2–3.
9. Office of Public Outreach and Communications, "SFUSD Facts at a Glance," http://www.sfusd.edu/en/assets/sfusd-staff/about-SFUSD/files/SFUSD%20Facts%20at%20a%20Glance%20(April%202014)%20FINAL.pdf.
10. Arden Bucklin-Sporer, interview by the author, May 1, 2014.
11. Life Lab, "Survey Says . . . School Gardens Thriving in California—Results from the California School Garden Survey" (press release), May 28, 2014, http://www.lifelab.org/wp-content/uploads/2013/12/Press-Release-California-School-Garden-Survey-5.28.2014.pdf.
12. The DC Healthy Schools Act 2014–2015 requirement is 75 minutes of health education and 150 and 225 minutes of physical education per week for elementary and middle school students, respectively; in addition, it encourages 60 minutes of physical activity each day for all grade levels.

Chapter 5
1. See Sharon Gamson Danks's book *Asphalt to Ecosystems: Design Ideas for Schoolyard Transformation* (Oakland, CA: New Village Press, 2010).
2. Sam Ullery, interview by the author, May 19, 2014.
3. Melanie LaForce and Liz Bancroft, *Science in the Schoolyard Evaluation: Final Report* (Chicago: Outlier Research and Evaluation, CMSE, University of Chicago, 2013), http://outlier.uchicago.edu/BSI-SSY/about-evaluation/.
4. Bridget Rodriguez, interview by the author, April 30, 2014.

Chapter 6
1. In response to the widespread sense that American schools were deteriorating, President Reagan's Secretary of Education Terrel Bell commissioned a report on the state of public education. *A Nation At Risk* was released in 1982 and was led by Secretary Bell and his committee of educators, business leaders, and government employees. They concluded, after eighteen months of looking at data ranging from test scores to letters from concerned parents, that student performance had deteriorated so far from previous decades and in relation to international peers that the situation was as calamitous as "an act of war" against the country, a self-inflicted "educational

disarmament." The commission cited evidence: international peers had surpassed America to such a degree that we were never in first or second place but notably "last seven times." A significant portion of American adults and children were functionally illiterate, including as much as 40 percent minority youth. Business leaders reported that American high school graduates were "neither ready for college nor for work." Noting the enormous cultural shift toward "one global village" and the advent of an "information age," the report called for fundamental educational reform to achieve "a fair chance for all children" and a society that encouraged and supported lifelong learning for all citizens. The report was brief, eloquent, and urgent. It galvanized the country and redirected education policy.

2. The legislation in 1994, the Improving America's Schools Act (reauthorization of the Education and Secondary Education Act, or ESEA), required states to establish standards for math and ELA, the same for students in all racial and economic subgroups, and to assess their progress in at least three grades (in third grade, eighth grade, and high school).

3. Mary Smoyers, interview by the author, December 18, 2013.

4. Sam Dillon, "Schools Cut Back Subjects to Push Reading and Math," *New York Times*, March 26, 2006, http://www.nytimes.com/2006/03/26/education/26child.html?pagewanted=all&_r=0.

5. Margaret Webb Pressler, "Schools, Pressed to Achieve, Put the Squeeze on Recess," *Washington Post*, June 1, 2006, http://www.washingtonpost.com/wp-dyn/content/article/2006/05/31/AR2006053101949.html.

6. Delaine Eastin, "Message from the State Superintendent of Public Instruction," in *A Child's Garden of Standards: Linking School Gardens to California Education Standards* (Sacramento: Nutrition Services Division, California Department of Education, 2002), v.

7. Rose Hayden-Smith, "The California 'Garden in Every School' Story" (paper presented at the Society of Nutrition Educators National Meeting, Chicago, Illinois, August 2007).

8. Jens Manuel Krogstad and Richard Fry, "Dept. of Ed. Projects Public Schools Will Be 'Majority-Minority' This Fall," Pew Research Center, August 18, 2014, http://www.pewresearch.org/fact-tank/2014/08/18/u-s-public-schools-expected-to-be-majority-minority-starting-this-fall/.

9. Lisa D. Delpit, *Other People's Children: Cultural Conflict in the Classroom* (New York: New Press, 1995).

10. Regents of the University of California, "Full Option Science System," http://www.fossweb.com/delegate/ssi-foss-ucm/ucm?dDocName=D567152.

11. Alice Waters, "Our Work," Edible Schoolyard Project, http://edibleschoolyard.org/node/102.

12. USDA Farm-to-School 2013 census.

13. Green Schools National Network, https://greenschoolsnationalnetwork.org/find-a-school.

14. Gerald A. Lieberman, *Education and the Environment: Creating Standards-Based Programs in Schools and Districts* (Cambridge, MA: Harvard Education Press, 2013).

Chapter 7
1. Next Generation Science Standards: "Human activities have significantly altered the biosphere, sometimes damaging or destroying natural habitats and causing the extinction of other species. But changes to Earth's environments can have different impacts (negative and positive) for different living things" (MS-ESS3-3); "Typically as human populations and per-capita consumption of natural resources increase, so do the negative impacts on Earth unless the activities and technologies involved are engineered otherwise" (MS-ESS3-3), (MS-ESS3-4); "Organisms, and populations of organisms, are dependent on their environmental interactions both with other living things and with nonliving factors" (MS-LS2-1).
2. Dilafruz R. Williams and P. Scott Dixon, "Impact of Garden-Based Learning on Academic Outcomes in Schools: Synthesis of Research Between 1990 and 2010," *Review of Educational Research* 83, no. 2 (2013): 226.
3. The IBM PC was introduced in 1981 and the original Apple Macintosh was introduced in 1984.
4. Magnavox Odyssey, released in 1972, was the first home video game console.
5. Dennis W. Chek, "Education About the History of Technology in K–12 Schools" (paper presented at the Annual Meeting of the Society for the History of Technology, Pasadena, California, October 15–17, 1997), 4.
6. National Center for Education Statistics, "Internet Access in U.S. Public Schools and Classrooms: 1994 – 2000," Statistics in Brief, Table 1, May 2001, http://nces.ed.gov/pubs2001/2001071.pdf.
7. Betsy Corcoran, "A Brief History of (Edtech) Time," *Texas Education Review* 1 (2013): 104–118.
8. Susan B. Neuman and Donna C. Celano, *Giving Our Children a Fighting Chance: Poverty, Literacy, and the Development of Information Capital* (New York: Teachers College Press, 2013).
9. As cited in Corcoran, "A Brief History": the Bill & Melinda Gates Foundation, the Hewlett Foundation, and the MacArthur Foundation.

Acknowledgments

It's been a great privilege to write this book. I've been captivated for many years now by how to make it possible for children to be in gardens, and it still seems to me one of the most important and valuable experiences children can know. I am grateful to the teachers I've met who have laid out the path for this simple yet ambitious vision through their work in the classroom and the garden. This book is dedicated to them, with a special acknowledgment to those who generously shared their stories with me for this book: Jamillah Bakr, Itonya Dismond, Janet Forté, Neal Klinman, Caitlin O'Donnell, Erica Pastor, Madhvi Patil, Donna Peruzzi, Kelly Petitt, Mary Smoyers, and Tory Tolles.

I am indebted to the science educators at the Cambridge Public Schools Department of Science, Technology, Engineering, and Math, the best collaborators in garden-based learning anyone could wish for: Susan Agger, Marianne Dunne, Dan Monahan, and Lisa Scolaro. They were the first people I turned to when I started this book because I knew I could count on their friendship, as well as their knowledge and experience, to help me tell this story.

Thank you to my peers in garden-based learning for the work they do to create ongoing opportunities for children's play and learning outside. Their experience—as I have understood it—has shaped my thinking (and this book), and I am particularly indebted to Arden Bucklin-Sporer, Whitney Cohen, Jeanne McCarty, Kristin Metz, Ross Miller, and Sam Ullery, who generously and candidly reflected on their hopes and challenges in the field.

My CitySprouts colleagues, past and present, bring true gold to the children, youth, teachers, and families we work with. The school garden program we've created together is so much more than the sum of any one person's effort. It has been an amazing experience to be part of it. I owe a special thanks to two CitySprouts friends (and former board members), Joe Petner and Bridget Rodriguez, for sharing their perspective on the CitySprouts story for this book.

To Paige Green, Cambridge Public Schools Superintendent Jeff Young, Laura Sewrey, Ross Miller, Sam Ullery (again), and the incredibly patient Alison Risso, I thank you for sharing the photographs, drawings, and documents that ground these program descriptions in a real context. I am indebted to friends and colleagues who read early versions of this work, directed me to sources for further reading, or shared perspectives, including Dean Blase, Kevin McGonegal, Abigail Norman, Neil Schiavo, and Henry Vandermark.

Thanks to Nancy Walser, my editor at Harvard Education Press, for her guidance and genuine interest in the work taking place in learning gardens. Lastly, I thank my wonderfully supportive friends and family for their encouragement, especially my husband, Tom, and my daughters, Anna Lee and Ursula, who started me on this venture into school gardens in the first place.

About the Author

Jane S. Hirschi is the founding director of CitySprouts, a school garden program that started in two Cambridge, Massachusetts, public schools in 2001 and now operates in twenty public schools in Cambridge and Boston.

Ms. Hirschi is a vocal champion for school gardens, particularly the need for garden-based learning in low-resourced, urban schools. She has spoken to—and written for—audiences as diverse as the business community, public school educators, parents, and children. She's planted a lot of gardens in her life, mostly small ones, and maintained a compost bin wherever she's lived. She now resides with her husband and two daughters in Cambridge.

Index

DATE DUE

PRINTED IN U.S.A.